Theatre in Education
New objectives for theatre—new techniques in education

For Gavin Bolton

Theatre in Education

New objectives for theatre—new techniques in education

John O'Toole

HODDER AND STOUGHTON
LONDON SYDNEY AUCKLAND TORONTO

ISBN 0 340 20617 9 Boards
ISBN 0 340 20618 7 Unibook

Printed and bound in Great Britain for
Hodder and Stoughton Educational,
a division of Hodder and Stoughton Ltd,
Mill Road, Dunton Green, Sevenoaks, Kent
by Richard Clay (The Chaucer Press) Ltd, Bungay, Suffolk

Contents

For about a decade, Theatre in Education (TIE) has been growing almost un-chronicled. The nervous reluctance of those who practise it to commit themselves to written description or definition springs from its origins and development. It was conceived as an attempt to bring the techniques of theatre into the classroom, in the service of specific educational objectives. From the beginning it maintained that its aim was more than generally to be entertaining and thought-provoking, or to encourage the habit of theatre-going (thus renouncing the traditional aims of children's theatre). It based itself on both an extension of children's play and a combination of theatricality and classroom techniques to provide an experience imaginative in its own right, with the glamour of strangers in dramatic role and costume providing both a stimulus and a context which are not normally available to the teacher.

From these roots have developed the techniques which give TIE its special identity. Firstly, the material is usually specially devised, tailor-made to the needs of the children and the strengths of the team. Secondly, the children are often asked to participate; endowed with roles, they learn skills, make decisions, and solve problems, so the programmes' structures have to be flexible (the actor/teachers no less so) to respond to the children's contributions within the context of the drama and still to uphold the roles. To create through this participation an involvement deep enough to be a significant aid to any learning process demands small audiences, usually just one or two classes, preferably in a localised area, ideally within a single community. Thirdly, teams are usually aware of the importance of the teaching context, and try to prepare suggestions for follow-up work, or to hold preliminary workshops for the class teachers; programmes are frequently split into two or three parts, to allow the teacher to build a large-scale project on the stimulus of the drama. This does not automatically imply academic pretension or solemnity; theatre in education programmes are exciting, and as funny, sad, magical, glamorous and novel as any other good theatre. These elements are harnessed to a serious educational purpose, perhaps to teach something as specific as road safety or languages, more often to kindle the imagination and awaken understanding of important issues, and to shake preconceptions.

Developing these techniques has been, and still is, an absorbing and risky process, inviting failure. In the early days, there was considerable enthusiasm from both teachers and the theatrical profession, often undiscriminating, occasionally cynical. A great deal of dedicated effort and experiment followed, along with unimaginative imitation, extremism, shoddy work, the deliberate and accidental exploitation of children and sponsors, and inevitable disillusion. As scepticism and hostility set in, so the purveyors of theatre in education became more defensive and more insular, frightened of being committed to anyone or anything that might prove compromising as they struggled to consolidate their positions, in the face of education committees and theatre boards who were less than enthusiastic at the cost of such a peripheral service.

It is increasingly being realised that such reticence only increases misunderstanding and distrust, a point repeatedly emphasised at the 1974 national Symposium in Theatre in Education, held in Leeds. This book is a preliminary attempt to define some of the rationale and describe some of the practice of it, without resorting to the jargon of the initiated. It is in no way intended to be comprehensive or definitive—theatre in education is mercifully too varied for that, and my own experience is limited and inevitably unrepresentative. It is the subjective analysis of a consumer, observer and part-time purveyor of theatre in education over five years. The opinions and perspectives are my own, and are those of an educationist rather than a theatre buff, subjugating artistic and theatrical dimensions to the needs of the real consumers, the children. If the book merely goads one of the many with more wisdom and experience in the field into writing a confutation of the views expressed here, it will have achieved something.

I would like to thank all the members of the following professional companies for their help and hospitality, and, where appropriate, for permission to quote or refer to their work: Billingham Forum Young People's Theatre; Birmingham Drama Centre; Bolton Octagon TIE; Cockpit TIE, London; Coventry Belgrade TIE; Dublin Abbey Theatre TIE; Flintshire TIE; Greenwich Bowsprit TIE; Leeds Playhouse TIE; Leicester Flying Phoenix TIE; Live Theatre, Tyneside; Liverpool Priority Everyman Community Theatre; Oxford Playhouse Team; Redbridge local education authority Team; Stockton

Dovecot Arts Centre; Theatre Centre, London; Tyneside Theatre Stagecoach; Wear-about, Sunderland.

My thanks are equally due to all the drama advisers, teachers and students concerned with TIE who have given assistance, in particular David Griffiths and the talented and dedicated amateurs of Durham and South Tyne Theatres in Education, working with whom has been so exciting over the past five years. Newcastle University and Durham County Education Authority together made the book possible with their kind award of a Schools Fellowship and secondment.

My most grateful tributes must go to Roger Chapman, whose programmes introduced me to theatre in education, and who has provided much sound advice since; and above all to Gavin Bolton, to whom this book is dedicated: I hope a little of his wise understanding of the dramatic needs of children may be reflected in it.

The help of all these people is indicative of the new feeling within the trade: there is now tacitly but definitely a theatre in education movement, well aware of its responsibilities and problems, realistic about its strengths and weaknesses—at last curious, not defensive, about its diversities of aim and practice. The movement is weak in bargaining power, and has enormous problems to solve inside and outside the classroom. Such public image as it has developed is contradictory, for the meddlers, dilettantes and those using it for ulterior motives have lost nearly as much public favour as the dedicated but reticent actor/teachers of quality have gained. The movement is, however, thoughtful and clearsighted, and it knows where it is going. At its best it is an exciting and valuable service to those local education authorities who have been far-seeing and loyal enough to support it through its infancy; now it is ready for a growth and expansion in which this book is just a step.

Chapter One

What it is and where it came from

Theatre in Education: the term is more specific than it looks, so for those who have never heard the phrase, as well as for those who know exactly what it means and wonder whether I do, it seems best to start with some concrete descriptions. From the three typical programmes described below some common elements emerge clearly, and some diversity is illustrated, too. It is, of course, impossible to convey by a verbal description of either a successful lesson or stage play the subtle process of communication between human beings which in the theatre is usually called atmosphere and in schools is occasionally recognised as education; the accounts below merely outline the structure and some of the external signs. The quality or magic of personal experience is missing —and that quality is the essence of theatre in education.

The Happy Land[1] (a programme for six to seven year olds, six to nines in special schools)

On the day of the performance the children receive a large, brightly-coloured envelope addressed to their class with a card inside inviting them to the birthday party of the Princess of The Happy Land, in her garden. The programme starts with a character dressed in purple and gold coming into the children's classroom, looking for them, he says. He introduces himself as the Princess's Chamberlain, Nolo. His character will vary according to what he has already learnt from the class teacher that the children can contribute; for instance, he can be forgetful and funny, calm and assured, or worried and fussy. Whatever character he chooses, he must also be someone in whom the children can believe and trust, their link with the security which adults provide in the precarious reality of their normal world, someone with whom they can enter the fantasy safely. When he judges them to be ready, he takes them along to the school hall, which is full of birdsong and music. Here they all sing and dance, preparing to meet the Princess. They practise the rituals of bowing and presentation, then one child is deputed to knock on the Palace door. To a fanfare, the Princess enters. She greets them warmly, and is delighted when they give her a birthday present of a little harp. Playing this, she sings with the children, then starts playing a noisy game of the children's limited choice, usually 'Musical Statues', or something similar and lively. During this, Nolo goes off.

A few moments later a great wind is heard, a black Wizard appears, angry that his peace has been disturbed, frightening the children and putting a complicated rhyming spell on the Princess:

> 'Ho Ho, Princess, no more joy
> Till you discover a magic toy;
> No more laughter, no more joy,
> No more smiles without this toy:
> A doll who can dance to music sweet,
> A doll with magic in her feet.'

He sweeps back to his hiding place, leaving the children alone with the withdrawn and weeping Princess. A long pause follows, while the children are left to feel the pull of conflicting emotions and react to the situation.

Eventually, when he judges the moment to be right, Nolo re-enters to ascertain from the children what has happened; together they try to make the Princess laugh or smile. As the children tell jokes, dance, or pull faces to please her, he goes off and fetches an old book of spells from the Palace. They all read through this, and discover the right spell at the end. Where can they obtain a magic doll? Sometimes the children's ideas are tried and nearly succeed; Nolo implants the idea of a Toymaker if the children do not suggest it. A real telephone system is located, and the children 'phone up the Toymaker. He answers that he just happens to have a doll ready which he will bring along, and he asks the children to call him so that he can find them in the Princess's garden. As soon as they start shouting, the Wizard and the wind re-appear, re-inforcing his spell on the Princess and his presence.

As he goes off back to his hideout, the Toymaker is blown in, a bright fantastical figure with an empty doll-stand in his hand. He blames or questions the children, and after finding out what has happened he suggests that the pieces of the doll must have been blown round the garden. The children hunt for the pieces, stowed round the hall in advance, and help the Toymaker to put the bits together, all singing his working song. The completed doll is life-size, but very unlifelike, and must be magicked alive.

The doll comes alive (*The Happy Land*)

The children invent a spell which they chant, with their eyes shut, before a curtain drawn in front of the doll. First and second times nothing happens (somebody must have been looking), but the third time (with the aid of a nearby door and an unobtrusive switch) the living doll is revealed, to the children's invariable relief and wonder. The Toymaker tries his keys and is just about to make the doll dance, when the Wizard reappears, snatches the keys, and goes to sit on top of his hideout, to keep an eye on the children.

Three groups are formed, led by the Princess, Nolo and the Toymaker, to invent a plan to retrieve the keys. The plans are tried in turn, with mounting tension; the third one (as a rule) works and the keys are recovered, along with the Wizard's magic powder, leaving him powerless, usually asleep. The doll is wound up, she dances, and the Princess smiles again. The last thing to decide is what to do with the Wizard; the characters disagree, so the children are left to make the decision, with the emphasis slanted (in the light of experience) towards a happy resolution. Everybody joins in a last happy dance, then the children say goodbye to the Princess. Nolo takes them back to the classroom, where he asks them to keep the Princess happy by painting her a picture of the story, and inviting them to write letters to any of the characters.

In this programme the children are quickly swept up in the action; they become entirely committed to the story, and the atmosphere throughout is of excited, lively and controlled activity. Both ingenuity and imagination are worked hard: the children vividly experience fear, frustration and sadness, but in the manageable and basically secure situation of group make-believe, where they can act out these emotions and where they are finally resolved. The experience is personal and co-operative, powerful and complete. It is also fun.

Ghost in the Village[2]

(a programme for one or two classes of eleven year olds, designed to fit in with local history work in Northumbria)

Part 1 The actors come to the school to give a short theatrical account of how a sailor in the nineteenth century brought back cholera to his remote fell village—which remains unnamed. During the play something of the village way of life is depicted, revolving round subsistence sheep-farming and crofting; the simple, superstitious religion of the people is emphasised, along with their distrust of outsiders and those who, like the sailor, have had dealings with the outside world. The outcome is not given, but above all the story is heroic, with each character selflessly pledging himself to do what is best for the community, at whatever personal risk. At the end, an actor comes forward as himself and gives the children a package, saying:

> 'Near here, in 1845, something like this really happened. Do you think the people then would have behaved like those in our play, as heroically? Here is some evidence discovered by archaeologists; see what you can make of it.'

Part 2 During the following week the children examine the evidence with their teacher, and write up their conclusions. The archive pack gives a plan of the village, still unnamed, and a local map. The pack is ambiguous, other details including a picture of a row of post holes apparently right round the village; a bone with a musket ball embedded in it; scraps of letters and diaries; a cut, apparently bloodstained piece of cloth; statistics of differing numbers of bodies found in various parts of the village; and so on. The evidence is complex and not obviously biased, but there are clear hints that all was not sweetness and heroic self-sacrifice.

Part 3 A week later the actors return and start a drama session with the children in the hall. Two actors each work with half the children, at opposite ends, representing the neighbouring villages of Thockrington and Bavington. Organising the children into family groups, the actors develop the concept of living in a tight-knit, simple community such as had been shown the week before, by preparing with the groups for the annual Two Villages sheep-shearing festival. Everybody prepares to contribute something. During the preparations, the sailor brother of the Thockrington champion shearer returns and is welcomed—both of these characters are actors. Work continues until playtime.

Part 4 After break the children return for the festival itself, which takes place in Thockrington amid much noise, music, dancing and fun. All the children make their contributions, leading up to the Grand Shearing contest. In this, performed in mime, it is noticed that the much-vaunted Thockrington champion is curiously below form. He suddenly collapses, violently ill. The old woman of Bavington (another actor), who is the only person in either village to understand medical matters, pronounces 'Cholera', and immediately calls all the people of Bavington back to their village.

In each village there is a consultation; this, the moral centre of the programme, is taken slowly and seriously, the actors emphasising in their roles the importance of the decisions facing the villages, feeding in the ideas and questions that will encourage deeper discussion, unobtrusively forcing the children to stretch further their understanding of implications. Eventually each village decides on a plan of action to cope with the crisis in its own interest. Then each village must find some way of communicating with the other. Finally, some joint decision is made and implemented, which may be agreement, compromise, or deadlock; the amount of collaboration and support, the amount of hostility and mutual exclusion, depend on the children. Sometimes the Thockringtonians voluntarily cut themselves off; sometimes the Bavingtonians stockade them in; sometimes a mutual aid plan is settled—the old woman of Bavington is a key figure in this, and how she role-plays is a powerful control. During this session the shearer dies, and his body is left, alone, at the end of the session.

Part 5 Back in the hall after lunch, the children's help is enlisted by an actor, speaking out of role, who explains that they are going to carry on the play in a different way, one that can only work with the children's help. The 'dead' character, he explains, will return as the 'Spirit of Cholera' and those whom he touches must fall ill. Anybody he touches twice will die; what is going to happen is what actually did happen in 1845. The actor emphasises that this dramatic ending cannot work if the children do not obey the rules of the game: that 'Cholera' cannot be seen, that it is useless to try running away from him or dodging his touch, that anybody touched must submit.

A short piece of theatre follows, during which 'Cholera' rises and touches the Thockrington sailor, who demonstrates how the children should react by looking ill and collapsing. While the children are still watching, 'Cholera' touches one of the children (who has been secretly briefed beforehand); he does the same. After this, according to what decision was taken at the end of the previous session, the action continues as improvised drama—usually including nursing, escape plots, heroic missions, panics, betrayals, deathbeds. Here, 'Cholera' is the silent control factor; he touches very few, even fewer twice. He may cross between villages behind a party of villagers or escapees, or withdraw unobtrusively when the action is ingenious and involved. Finally he steps forward dramatically and calls in an imperious voice brooking no interruption:

'Silence and be still! All be still and see the fate of the villages. All whom I touch now will die. Nobody else shall move. Be still and see your destiny!'

Unhurriedly but purposefully he moves among the people of Thockrington, touching each of them twice, but ignoring those from Bavington. As he does so, the tape recorder is switched on, and a voice reads quietly the parish register of the dead, including their ages, to show how many children also died. The five actors go quietly out, leaving the recorder playing.

Part 6 The teacher takes the children, by coach, to Thockrington, where the church still stands, and the village is quite visible as grassy mounds in a field (owned by a helpful farmer who knows the story). While they are there the teacher points out that, so far as is known, the whole population was wiped out, the village was abandoned, and there are in fact no official records at all, the evidence for Part 2 having been made up to help the play. Why are there no records?

Though this programme is a 'documentary' of local history, its aim was never merely documentation, either of nineteenth-century village life in Northumberland, or even of the effect of cholera on a community. It tries, through the use of dramatic conflict and theatrical role-play, to give children some understanding of the complex interplay of self-interest and selflessness, expediency and heroism, compassion and fear, in a moral and physical crisis. Such understanding can only be learnt by being felt. It is not gay fun, like the first programme, but children of this age have a passion for serious even morbid enquiry, and the ability to comprehend complex moral issues if presented in concrete terms as part of a 'reality' they can recognise.

The Ballad of Billy Martin[3] (a programme for up to fifty senior pupils in secondary schools)

This programme, much more obviously theatrical than the other two described, also takes place in the school hall, but it is blacked out, and the students sit recognisably as an audience half in the round, with most of the action taking place in front of them. There are complicated sound effects and a lighting plot. Before coming in, the students have been looking at an exhibition of blown-up photographs of down-and-outs, together with an anthology of short poems and articles, serious and humorous, about them.

The performance starts with a guitarist in spotlight who starts singing a song, to the tune of 'Streets of London', about a young man with ideals. The lights go up on a derelict site, with three destitutes; a scuffle over a meths bottle, followed by a muted confrontation with the police that achieves little for anybody, results in one of them, Billy, being left alone on stage—still a stereotype, scruffy, inarticulate, unintelligent and truculent, but beginning to be recognisably a sympathetic character—alone with his reverie. With sudden bright lights, loud music, applause and bonhomie equally artificial, a travesty of 'This is Your Life' takes place, flashing through the characters in Billy's past, whose brief comments are disconcerting, but as yet have little meaning. The last of these figures turns out to be the same policeman, who steps into Billy's fantasy, the lights and the compère fade out and Billy sees the beautiful scrapbook he has just been given, revealed as full of blank pages, follow his meths bottle into the dustbin.

The folk singer returns, providing continuity and setting the scene, as he does frequently in the programme's fragmented structure. The next scene paints a grimly amusing picture of Billy's family life, which he left prematurely. After this a Headmaster endows the audience as his careers class, and starts teaching them. Billy comes in, late again, and sits among them, disruptive from the start. The Head is called away, and he asks a confident member of the audience to look after the class. Billy causes a disturbance, the Head's glasses are broken, and the audience, who by this time have considerable sympathy with Billy, are forced to choose between him and their colleague as the Head demands to know the culprit. In any case, Billy is eventually punished.

Next he steals a teddy bear for his sister's child, and is thrown out of her house. He ends up in care, where the broad-minded but insensitive warden leaves him a free choice which he is ill-equipped to make without help, on the issue of sorting out Billy's latest miscalculation by either marriage, cohabitation, or abortion:

'Life, Billy, is like a fairground: what you lose on the roundabouts you gain on the swings.'

A fairground fantasy sequence is used to underline Billy's dilemma. Predictably, Billy chooses headlong flight, and the rest of the play traces his inexorable descent, in a collage of naturalistic episodes interspersed with silent-film style pantomime in stroboscopic light. This all finally accelerates to a powerful symbolic climax, where the pressures on Billy combine to thrust him down on to the derelict site where we first saw him.

The audience members are given five minutes, in groups, to formulate questions they would like to put to the characters. A seat is placed facing the audience, and they call up the characters whom they wish to question, one at a time. The actors answer, in role. In all cases they try to force the questioners and the audience in general to think more deeply, giving short shrift to facile questions and easy attitudes. If the students are disposed to identify unthinkingly with Billy as a victim, the figures around him show their sympathetic side and their own problems; if the mood is priggishly to blame Billy for his own downfall, the emphasis is reversed.

All this is a preparation for the next drama lesson, when the students will be asked to explore in creative drama some of the positive aspects of the story. Who might have helped Billy, how and when? What could be done for him now? How can the problem of people like Billy be solved? What attempts at a solution are being made?

These three programmes have in common a number of immediately obvious factors:
all take place in schools;
all comprise a group of actors, working in role and in costume, for and with children;
each play, like any other, centres round definable characters in a state of dramatic conflict;
all involve areas of theatricality and performance combined with areas where the members of the audience are directly and personally spoken to, even personally embroiled in the dramatic conflict;
the subject matter of each play is clearly relevant to part of the curriculum in most English schools (imaginative story-telling in the infants' school, local history research projects for eleven-year-olds, exploration of social problems by senior pupils);
each has a specifically educational aim.

They are by no means representative of the considerable diversity of work in theatre in education; however, they reflect one line, perhaps the main line, of development in the field; they contain many of the strengths and weaknesses of much contemporary work. There is plenty of overlap with neighbouring areas of both theatre and education, producing mutual growth and sometimes mutual distrust. To clarify the position of theatre in education among the jargonistic maze of worthy if fashionable movements —the children's theatre movement, speech and movement, the movement movement, young people's theatre, youth theatre, theatre workshops, school plays, educational drama, creative dramatics, *et alia*—it might be helpful to trace its origins.

Theatre in education is usually regarded as starting in the middle 'sixties, though its origins are earlier, rooted in a number of only loosely related activities. Most obviously, but not the prime mover, was the development of children's theatre. In America, for example, since the turn of the century plays specially written for children have been performed by actors committed to this work at an increasing level of sophistication and organisation: a network of resident companies, usually linked to University drama departments, often with fine auditoria of their own. The roots of this activity, in turn, go back deep into the history of theatre. In England, progress has been more informal; a few professional companies, such as Bertha Waddell's from the nineteen-twenties, the Young Vic of Esmé Church, and more recently the Unicorn Theatre in London, have been formed, whose aims are in some senses broadly but not primarily educational, to educate children toward a love of the theatrical experience, or to stimulate their imaginations: 'To entertain, to give an enjoyable time and to provoke thought' (Ursula Jones, The Unicorn Theatre). In almost all areas of England there are amateur groups, usually either made up of teachers, like the Hampshire Children's Theatres, or attached to Amateur Dramatic Societies; most of them are convened occasionally or seasonally, to bring theatre to children.

An offshoot of this movement, and a factor in the development of theatre in education, is the number of companies who exist to take theatre into schools at a professional level; usually touring companies, but occasionally attached to repertory theatres, they perform scripted plays, or parts of plays. In primary schools, these are frequently fairy tales or legends, and there is usually a high fantasy content; in secondary schools, the aim is to bring schoolchildren into contact with great or at least good literature and examination syllabuses are often consulted to discover what set texts are being 'done', and these are then presented in a way intended to bring Shakespeare or Shaw off the printed page.

In recent years, too, live theatre has played its part: theatre directors, grimly aware of the lure of other media, and conscious of the need to cater for a wider public by improving theatre's narrowly classbound image, have made a determined set at school-children, the next generation of paying customers. Or, to put it charitably, many people in the theatre, reflecting the more egalitarian post-war outlook, are striving to give more and more people a taste of the power of theatre. In an attempt to replace in young people's minds theatre as a Christmas treat with the concept of theatre as an exciting and stimulating experience for all, many theatres are going to the people if the people will not go to them.

These forces from the world of theatre have converged with another group of forces, perhaps even more dynamic—changing concepts of education. New understanding of learning processes has led first to a search for new, more stimulating ways of presenting and adapting the curriculum content. Gradually in turn this is leading to changing concepts of the nature and function of education itself; a radically altered vision of the educational process demands a new relationship between the school and the learner. It is no longer a question of finding new, more efficient techniques to supersede the old; now many of the techniques, school and classroom structures, and relationships of the traditional 'knowledge-banking' or 'skill-developing' systems are irrelevant and obstructive to the 'growth-based' and 'problem-solving' theories being dangled in front of teachers by educationists. To implement them, teachers are improvising, experimenting, casting around often in the dark for new curricula, a new role and new techniques to catch the elusive trout of 'relevance', 'community awareness', 'communication skills'.

Among the leaders in this philosophical scramble have been the practitioners of educational drama. Drama has long had a foothold in schools as part of 'Literature'. The school play has been encouraged or at least tolerated as much for the aura of cultural heritage it confers on the status of the school as for the training it gives in skills of performance, co-operative activity and public confidence. Largely since the Second World War, a genuinely new concept of drama as an educational tool has emerged. Pioneered by Peter Slade and the post-war breed of local education authority drama advisers, rationalised in colleges and Universities by such people as Dorothy Heathcote, Gavin Bolton and John Hodgson, made respectable by an H.M.I. official report, it has above all been practised and refined in the schools themselves. This drama is very much influenced by the realisation of the educative and exploratory nature of children's own games, and it draws more on the dramatic content and experience of children's play than on adult drama. Situations of dramatic conflict, imaginative projection and role-play are set up to help children explore through improvisation the problems and possibilities of their identity, their surroundings, other people and the interplay of all three.

Improvisation had already been used for many years in the theatre, sometimes extensively, sometimes tentatively, but mainly for two rather different reasons. Firstly, it was used to prepare an actor, to help to train him in aspects of his technique, or in his ability to understand texts in general, and to develop his sensitivity towards other actors. Secondly, it was used to explore the dramatic implications of a particular text, scene, or crux as a specific preparation for doing it justice in interpretation. Many years ago Goethe suggested, but few since have explored, another function: the use of improvisation as a means of inventing situations to explore, which either (*a*) have an already real basis in the participants' experience, in order to provide greater understanding, or (*b*) are real, but not experienced, in order to discover what is comprehensible and relatable. This gives drama a new dimension, and recently it has been seized on eagerly by psychologists and sociologists along with teachers. The teacher in a drama lesson of this kind sets up a context of vicarious experience for the children, who become the subjects of the learning process, selecting and controlling the learning objects. He may have to structure or deepen the involvement and the direction of the process, but to do this he must be sensitive to the individual and corporate energies within the improvisation, without destroying the continuity of the dramatic experience. Where better than from inside, and teachers themselves started to learn to role-play. However, class teachers can provide an understanding of the needs of their individual pupils, but they cannot provide the freshness of novelty and a different angle, the stimulus of theatricality and glamour.

At this point these two progressive forces in theatre and education met, reacted, and fused into an element that was at first insignificant but essentially new and different.

They had touched once or twice previously, in an exploratory way. As early as 1937 Glasgow's Director of Education (at first cautiously, later enthusiastically) allowed Bertha Waddell's company to perform in junior schools, in school time, free of charge. Soon after the Second World War, Aberdeen Education Authority created and sponsored a team of speech and drama specialists to work in schools, employing techniques of both educational drama and live theatre. Companies formed around the same time in Birmingham and London were conscious of the educational possibilities of follow-up work and co-operation with the school system. Peter Slade's Pear Tree Players claimed to be the first theatre company entirely devoted to education. A little later Brian Way stated formally that the *second* of the three aims of his company was to assist teachers in all types of schools with methods of approach to drama in education. This company was in the forefront of early experiment with children's direct participation in a theatrical experience.

A muffled explosion came in the mid-'sixties. The new educational forces sought and found in theatre the dynamic medium they had been looking for. Coventry's civic theatre, the Belgrade, in consultation with teachers and backed by the local education authority, established, at first as a pilot scheme, 'a performing company committed to an audience (of young people) for a single session, licensed to stimulate ideas and images by whatever methods connect here, now.'

The work, for which they coined the term 'Theatre in Education', was designed to operate within the school system, and was seen as important in its own right.

'We do not aim to create the social habit of theatre—it is an imaginative experience in its own right, an extension of the games children play in everyday life.'

The material used was to be tailor-made, original:

'A group of people define an aim, devise material to communicate that aim, then present the project using drama and theatre skills ... to relate to the moment of commitment not the technical intricacies of production.'[4]

Within the next few years companies were formed in places as dissimilar as Bolton and Bournemouth, Greenwich and Flintshire. There was enormous initial enthusiasm, both from a theatrical profession looking about equally for new modes of artistic expression and new bread tickets; and from those teachers, desperate or idealistic and frequently both, who were struggling to follow the light of progressive ideas through the fog of academical disapproval and pupils' low expectations, and who seized on TIE with uncritical delight. This delight was often as short-lived as the poorer companies, and the resulting disillusion has made national acceptance harder for the thoughtful and dedicated teams.

The picture now is of unsteady, slow growth and expansion on a number of fronts. A terminology has evolved, starting with the ubiquitous abbreviation *TIE*.

'The terms "lesson" and "stage play" are replaced by the word *programme* as the experience will probably incorporate different and sometimes a greater variety of communication methods than will either the traditional lesson or the traditional play' (Cora Williams, Bolton TIE).

These *programmes* are the staple product of TIE companies of all kinds. Coventry's original 'single session' is more and more being superseded as the links with schools grow; the lasting value of the 'one-off' seems little, the follow-up work often limited and even stultifying, compared with what can be achieved by multiple visits connected with curricular projects. The *teams* (that is, those who practise TIE) need to have the communication skills of both teacher and actor (the controlled energy, understanding of his medium, absorption, projection and sensitivity to both audience and colleagues of the good actor; the sensitivity to children, ability to be absorbed and project that absorption, understanding of his medium and controlled energy of the good teacher). Accordingly they are called with heavy accuracy *actor/teachers*. In programmes where the children participate actively, if they are given roles involving characterisation this is known as *endowment*.

As much of the work involves a close and personal approach to the audience, where the children are often asked to make a direct personal contribution, audiences are usually small, one or two classes, and the work usually takes place in the school itself. There are no dogmas, however; many groups feel it is part of their function to produce theatre spectaculars for audiences of eight hundred; productions of set texts for examinations; animated physics lessons; youth theatre workshops; revues for college students; entertainments for youth clubs; street theatre.

Companies are variously constituted and the type of work varies accordingly, with each group emphasising and building on its relative strengths.

(*a*) Still in the van are the locally-based companies of full-time professionals, attached to a repertory theatre yet working independently, backed partly at least by education authority grants, providing a regular service in a prescribed area.

(*b*) Some 'fringe' companies, independent of establishment and often politically committed in a narrower or wider sense, undertake TIE as part of their whole scheme of work for the community.

(*c*) A few authorities have set up arts or drama centres where a mainly resident team

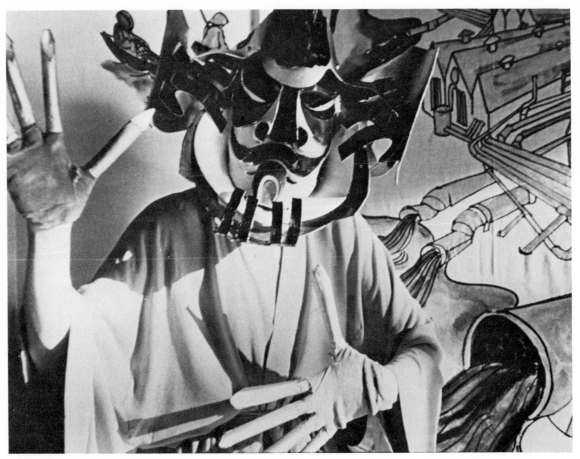

A powerful image from Coventry (*This Rare Earth*)

works on projects with local children sent for a day or half a day, using educational drama and TIE.

(*d*) There is a fluctuating number of established touring companies of different kinds, who visit areas on an occasional basis, giving single performances in as many schools as they can cover.

(*e*) Groups of drama specialists are employed by an education authority to undertake theatre in education part time; for the rest of the time they teach educational drama, school-based or peripatetic.

(*f*) Many colleges, departments and institutes of education make TIE a voluntary or compulsory part of their Drama or English courses for teachers, for the practical experience it gives the students of meeting and dealing with children in dynamic situations.

(*g*) Secondary schools themselves, even, sometimes encourage their sixth form or C.S.E. drama classes to prepare TIE programmes for their contemporaries or juniors.

(*h*) In addition there are groups of teachers dotted around the country trying to cover in their spare time the 95 per cent of schoolchildren at present unexposed to TIE.

Some companies undertaking this kind of work do not regard themselves as engaged in theatre in education. Deep-seated assumptions often make them nervous about education, or they feel that for a member of an audience theatricality and direct personal involvement are incompatible, that to experience both together weakens the impact of either. They usually declare their primary aim to be that of 'entertaining', or giving an 'exciting theatrical experience', so even when their material is curricular or drawn from literature, they work to that aim. They prefer to be called by more general terms, such as 'Children's Theatre' or 'Theatre for Young People'.

There is, of course, much overlap, both ways. The distinguishing feature of TIE is that *its overall primary aim is always educational*. It is continuing to develop aspects of the communication between teacher and learner—aspects such as role-play, imaginative projection and interaction, surprise and novelty, atmosphere and suspense, spectacle and theatricality. The elements themselves are well-known; the blend is genuinely new, taking tentative steps towards that fusion of the subjectivity and objectivity of understanding, cognitive, intuitive and emotional, which is the dream of the educationists. Whatever the product is called, that is the end; theatre is the means to that end.

Chapter Two

Theatrical and dramatic dimensions

The dual origins of TIE render it necessary to be specific about the nature of the experiences it offers. Basically, certainly, the aim is presentation; as in all theatre, a make-believe situation is performed to an audience. This may be as far as it goes, and many TIE programmes are designed to be presented to a passively involved receptive audience, seated in a school hall or in a theatre, using the dramatic power of the content and the theatrical power of the medium to achieve their educational objectives.

The development of educational drama has added a further possibility: the involvement of the audience, to a greater or lesser degree, in the action—their *participation*. This involvement may be vocal or physical, or both; it may be as helpers or extra performers, yet it does not change the essential nature of the experience. It can, however, add another dimension: the children may be integrally involved in the play itself, playing parts not only important to the structure, but also crucial to the dramatic conflict, becoming characters acted upon, reacting and actively influencing the continuation of the play. Both of the junior programmes already described (pages 1–7) use this kind of participation. The children may be involved as themselves, as in *The Happy Land*, or endowed with characters within which they can react naturally, as Roman children, for example, or as members of a fictitious youth club; sometimes they may be asked to project the appropriate reactions of a more complex characterisation, as Norman soldiers, perhaps, or as the villagers of Thockrington—whatever the roles, they may be protagonists or antagonists, victims or heroes. The children may have a further impact on the play, by being allowed to take over the playwright's role; the outcome may be constructed to depend on schemes they make and decisions they take.

Most of this book will be devoted to this kind of programme; though pure presentation, as I have indicated, may have the attributes which define it as TIE, this quality of harnessing the children's desire to be actively involved in an experience created for them and with which they identify, by integral participation, seems to me to be the really significant contribution that the TIE movement has made to the field of theatre. Where the active involvement affects the course of the play, the nature of the experience changes. The discovery and identification reach a new level: the situation may be make-believe, but the action, the happening, is real.

Looking at it from the obverse, this is closer to the experience of educational drama, and, originally, of children's play. Children in their own dramatic play act out stories and explore worlds where the outcome is in their hands; they create their own conventions: 'You've got to lie down, you're dead.' They use what they understand of adult convention and, though they have fantasy to fall back on, are not satisfied (and as they grow older they are increasingly less so) with easy, fantasy solutions. We must all have seen children externalising their fears and anxieties by playing bears, exploring the implications of conflict and morality in games of cowboys and Indians, learning to copy adult behaviour playing Mummies and Daddies—and sometimes doing all three at once (children in wartime will endlessly play fighters and bombers, tanks and ambushes). All the time they are unconsciously developing their ability to co-exist and work co-operatively, discovering and extending the limits of mutually acceptable behaviour, learning about leaders and roles, acceptance and rejection; often with tears, exasperation and boredom.

The function of educational drama is to extend, deepen and make more efficient this learning process, and as much as possible remove these last three factors (though exasperation, properly channelled, can be a powerful dramatic force!). The teacher's role is to take and organise the children's basic ideas into a framework that is satisfying in process as the children make and see their ideas develop to highlight the learning point or points. He must select the particular aim from the contribution the children are making, according to his knowledge of them. He may provide a starting point; he may feed in ideas or unexpected factors which will keep the class extended and absorbed.

This, the other end of the continuum expressed opposite, is not theatre in education, however, because the experience of presentation is missing, which implies that the experience of being an audience is missing too.

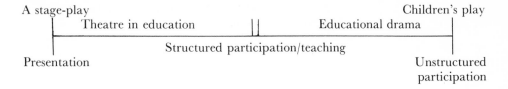

The teacher who role-plays in response to a need arising in the drama lesson does not automatically become an actor/teacher, though if he uses this technique to initiate a drama, for example by striding into the classroom at the beginning of the lesson in a burnous announcing that he is Jesus returning, he is taking a big step towards it. He is bringing to the children a context that is his, not theirs, asking them to share a game with his rules; before they can act they must observe, discover the conventions, and be acted upon to a degree where they can identify with the drama or characters, and so suspend their disbelief to react with a positive emotional and intellectual response. This is the function of an audience.

At this point the distinction between the two words 'drama' and 'theatre', as they are used in this book, becomes clear and needs to be made. Since children have no dramatic heritage, experience, or preconceptions to fall back on, it is necessary for anyone working in this field to clarify the fundamentals. By 'drama' I refer to the internal process, by 'theatre' essentially to the externals (though the two are and always have been Siamese twins, and to separate them is as dangerous as trying to separate content and form in any art).

Drama may be defined as the symbolic representation at first hand of the working out of relationships involving human beings. The process is dynamic, not static, and inevitably contains tension, as conflicts of interest, of emotional and intellectual need, are worked out. Though experienced at first hand, the symbolisation removes it from reality; here lies the security that an experience one knows to be drama can offer: one can always go home, reassert one's disbelief; there are no consequences. News media abound with dramatic and theatrical metaphors ('tragic mistake', 'dramatic rescue', 'Commons farce') which reflect the closeness of drama to reality in our lives, where in any case we cannot live without symbolisation. However, the roles we play in our own lives, by selectively presenting images of ourselves (postures and personae) to cope with our own social interaction, we have to sustain. We have to put up with embarrassment or humiliation if the posture we have chosen is inappropriate to the status with which we are endowed in the interaction, and sort out for ourselves the conflicts we create.

To take another example, what James Saunders has called 'the Theatre of Reality', public theatrical gestures may be 'staged', such as happened at the 1968 Olympic Games, where a champion sprinter, Tommy Green, standing on the Victory rostrum where it is normal to wave to the crowds gave instead the clenched fist salute of the Black Power movement: certainly symbolic, certainly in public for an audience, but as this was real life the actor was banned for life from the athletics stage for doing it. A movement in adult theatre is attempting to break down this tenuous barrier of the irresponsibility of drama; in children's theatre the issue becomes very problematic, for the younger the child, the less able he is to differentiate between fantasy and reality, and the more important a part of his real life is his play. It is quite possible, therefore, to present drama which the child believes to be real, and to which he will react as if to reality.

Physical presence or implied presence is essential to drama, for the first-hand perception of the relationship symbolised. A novel may be dramatic, but it is not drama; a playscript does not become drama until it is acted out—the ambivalence of the words act, act out, actually express this necessity. No representation can exist without an immediate awareness of the symbolic process being communicated. The acting out of the process may take a number of forms. Awareness may come with direct participation in the symbolised relationship in improvisation: educational drama, drama therapy, creative dramatics, socio-drama, structured role-playing—the names are many. It may be perceived by an audience through a selective medium, such as film, television or sound radio. Finally, it may be presented to the audience using all the dimensions of physical perception, with flesh and blood characters performing the action in front of, or among, the audience. This is theatre.

To a children's audience, it is the characters who define the experience as theatrical; they see figures whom they identify with roles in a context. Hence the initial importance of the actor as a stranger, or nearly so. It is easy to believe in an actor as a Cavalier soldier if your only experience of him is appearing like this, in great boots, lace cuffs, with martial bearing and a voice like thunder full of 'thou's'. It becomes a little harder, and requires a greater effort to suspend disbelief, if you recognise, under the helmet and bluster, last year's comic villain, and many actor/teachers know the moment of panic when they have impressively announced: 'I am Prince Rupert's Master of Horse', or some such role, and a perplexed but logical and very loud voice complains, 'No, you're not, you're Dennis the Duck.'

Of course, after a while, the dissociation between an actor and his part becomes clear, the convention is established just as with adults, and the identification becomes easier still, because the actor is *expected* to take up a role, even multiple roles, and the audience is prepared. To forestall this problem, some teams introduce themselves to the audience in advance as actors. 'Hello, I'm Jim, and this is Hazel, and Fred; we're from the X theatre in education, and we're going to perform a play for you.'

This attempt to establish the convention brings its own problems, though. First, it can remove some of the important surprise elements from the play, or at least weaken them. Secondly, with young children, for whom actor and character alike are exciting, undifferentiated ideas, it can bring its own brand of confusion. 'I am Prince Rupert's . . .' 'No, you're not, you're Jim.'

This necessary unfamiliarity is where the teacher is really unable to compete. The children's close knowledge of him and his behaviour inevitably lacks the glamour, the surprise and the exciting unpredictability of watching or working with strangers. In practice, theatre in education is bound to be an occasional, rare, or sometimes unique experience.

If it is the characters who make the experience theatrical, then the most crucial element to sustain the theatricality is the consistency of the characterisation. If the actors play several parts, each must be clearly different, and the actor must never slip from the behaviour which is appropriate to the role. This may seem obvious enough for a stage play; where participation by the children is involved, it brings both challenge and reward. In a programme invoking the children's response and using their ideas, much of the action and dialogue have to be unscripted, and it is easy to leave a role insufficiently developed, or to drop out of it, adopting instead of role a generalised attitude of adult dominance, or vague helplessness, or comfortable supportiveness. These are attitudes which are in the repertoire of the teacher, part of his function: the actor's job is to make them specific, give them an individual personality, or the experience becomes team teaching—valuable, perhaps, but not TIE. In addition, the actor's role carries one great advantage over the teacher—an advantage that teachers recognise as desirable, but rarely achieve. A natural discipline exists within the structure of a play. All well-constructed programmes have built-in controls, and all the actor has to do is manipulate the controls to obtain disciplined commitment. This takes great skill, of course, and continuous sensitivity on the actor's part to the dynamics of the group, especially as he does not know the children. In its way, this is part of the advantage; his very strangeness invokes diffidence, and his role brings authority, freed from its corollary, humiliation, by involvement in the story. For instance, a group of children, endowed as citizens of London in 1666, were pretending to fight the Great Fire.[5] Their uncontrolled and sloppy mime clearly indicated to the actor/teacher directing operations that their commitment to the situation was superficial, so in a pause he said loudly to a little girl, 'That's your house, isn't it?', and the level deepened perceptibly as the children now fought to save *Janice's* house. One child continued to play around in a silly way, so the actor turned on him sharply, with: 'If you throw buckets around like that, you'll have the water over me as well.' No more was needed; sheepish, but not humiliated, the boy joined in with a will.

All this implies that the other aspects of successful theatre are there. The novelty of being confronted by strange actors dressed in costume and talking like pirates or policemen can catch attention, but cannot sustain it *in vacuo*. Children's requirements as an audience (or rather audiences, because each age has different requirements) are in many ways more particular than adults'. It is necessary to be clear about the nature of the experience one is giving them, for nothing can be taken for granted; they themselves have little or no background of theatre to cushion the experience or relate it to; each moment stands or falls on what it can offer. Children are immediately willing to identify completely with what is offered and to make great efforts for it, or to reject it completely if it seems confusing or dull. Anyone bringing a theatre experience to young children must be very aware of his responsibilities; their eclectic impressionability is wide open to abuse by those who cloak ulterior motives or empty nothings in plausible spectacle. Their emotions are close to the surface, easy to tap, and they have no touchstones to use in discrimination. Moreover, they are nearly always a captive audience. If in school, like most happenings there it is arranged for them by their teachers; if in a theatre, it is the parents who buy the tickets. Children can rarely indulge the luxury of walking out, so their only refuge is inattention. To them, tedium is about the only sin. What is happening is tedious if they do not understand the motive, the material

All absorbed in the mime (*The Fire of London*)

or its relevance to something which touches their experience; it is also likely to be tedious if it is unvaried.

The dramatic content must be clear: a strong storyline is important, particularly for young children, and the focus of attention should be clear throughout. Children want to know the reason why things are happening, and the end in view must be one whose value they can recognise and relate to their own experience or feelings, especially where participation is made use of. All crises and moral issues in the drama must be made meaningful by being made concrete. Being members of a food-gathering tribe in a primitive village meant little to the eleven-year-olds in one programme,[6] even though they were supposed to be the children of the tribe (they knew *that*, hadn't they been told?) so the programme was put back on the drawing board, completely revised, and in subsequent performances the actor/teachers, as village elders, introduced them to the skills of hunting and of nursing the wounded. These particular activities were chosen bearing in mind the predilections of this age group in drama lessons. For half an hour the actor/teachers worked in mime with the children, teaching them in detail how to make good spears, stalk prey, and so on. All this was within the framework of the play; the children had to learn these skills in order to be initiated as young adults in the great ceremony soon to be held. The elders were difficult to please, and worked the children hard. The children were unfailingly fascinated by their activities, and became strongly committed to the life and problems of the village. Later, the actors wanted to make the children realise the implications of a water shortage in the village, so they, literally, *realised* the implications by going off, leaving the children alone with one bowl of water, and strict injunctions that as it was the last bowl it was not to be touched under any circumstances. Two kind and friendly strangers then arrived, desperate for water. The 'strangers' rarely had to take any part more active than being the objects of the resulting argument, as the children discovered for themselves the moral issues. So the function of the action in TIE is to take the generalised thematic objective, and make it selective, specific and concrete.

As children grow older, more complexities may be woven into the plot, but the focus must still be kept clear. It is easy to obscure all the issues by not separating them out and making the priorities plain. One recent programme* set out to explore for teenagers some of the themes implicit in legends of vampires. A spectacularly theatrical programme, carried out with great skill and panache, it nevertheless just failed to hold its audience, many of whom were not really sure what it had been about. Several of the themes possible to extract from the subject had been brought out and given an airing; the audience were asked to consider in turn, then together, the nature of the supernatural, the problem of facing up to death, the nature of evil, the archetypal power of legend, the moral problems of possessing extra-sensory powers, problems of conflicting lovers, family responsibilities, the consequences of individual action and the question of Destiny, besides being treated to a Pirandellian excursion through several layers of 'reality', as the characters stepped in and out of a play-within-a-play. Any one of these themes could have given the audience food for thought, perhaps more than one of them if kept clearly delineated and in proportion. What happened was that in the philosophical tangle of loose motifs to be explicated at the end, the pace dropped from the sparkling expository to the crawling tendentious, finally moralysis set in and the audience turned away to bait an unpopular teacher. This was a great pity, for the potential power of that material to stimulate young adolescents is limitless, and the use the programme made of the minor and secondary elements of theatricality was expert and confident; the programme had an ingenious structure, economical dialogue, contrasts of masked grotesquerie and credible naturalism, suspense, humour, and well-performed songs. Perhaps the structure was too ingenious: the function of structure in a TIE programme must be to focus the children's attention on the material of the programme in a way clear to them, which deepens their understanding and their attention. Nothing more. This makes it vitally important to understand children closely, and to know how and for how long they will react at a particular age to a particular stimulus. For this part of the planning of the programme the help of somebody with experience of working with children is indispensable.

The description of the last programme referred by implication to the concept of a distinction between primary and secondary theatricality, which perhaps needs clarification.

As *primary* elements I would include:

dramatic content—in practice inseparable from its casing:
the expression of the progression of the drama—that is, the action whether in the form of storyline or a sequence of ideas and images;

its structure—that is, the way the progression is ordered through the use of the
two primary media, language and movement;
the expression of the essence of the conflict, moment by moment, in these two media,
and in the characterisation; and
integral participation.

Secondary theatricality includes all the other elements of the spectacle, such as the
background and setting of the action, the stylistic mode, decorative effects such as song
and dance, visual and aural effects, and non-integral participation.

The use of integral participation as a primary factor can go a long way towards making
a display of 'pure' (secondary) theatricality much more than empty show. In one series
of visits to junior schools, a student group of actors, in role and concentrating particularly
on movement as something of an end in itself, assisted the children to create a 'Butterfly
Ball'[7]—a performance in which they all shared on the last visit, participating as various
members of the insect world preparing for a celebration dinner and dance. There seems
to have been little or no central dramatic content, yet there is small doubt that the
children, while thoroughly enjoying the experience as theatre, were extended in all sorts
of ways that the most suspicious educationist would accept, in the participation and
in the connected art, craft and writing which they also enjoyed.

Some of those most responsible for building up and supporting theatre for children
in Britain view the spread of theatre in education with much the same enthusiasm
as the Wedding Guest viewed the Ancient Mariner. In a magazine article (modified
slightly in a subsequent edition) the General Secretary of the British Children's Theatre
Association spoke for many.

'Much of it (a Festival of Young People's Theatre) was educationally most useful,
but miles away from the colour and life of the theatre ... it made a closer contact
between education and theatre possible ... but ... it does seem a pity if children
are to be everlastingly educated, in the name of theatre, through documentaries
whether situated in the mills or the mines or out on the open sea without being
brought into contact with the art of the theatre.... We thank God for the Christmas
pantomime when they will dance up and down with sheer delight and natural spontaneous participation' (Gerald Tyler).[8]

This and other attacks along the lines that theatre should be entertainment not education seem to have underlying them some linked assumptions that are both naive and untrue. The first (a myth often encountered in the theatre world) is that education is necessarily dull and undramatic, and ought to be left that way or it will transmit its contagious tedium; further, that the use of theatre to provoke thought on serious subjects is inviting this dullness (are King Lear, Major Barbara, or Mother Courage dull?); moreover, that the glamour of the theatre consists solely of 'magic' and 'fun'. Children of all ages have a great capacity for serious absorption in a serious subject, and being both enter- tained and excited by it, if it is rightly presented, so therefore in trying to plead for a cause, and very wisely warning us against the danger of untheatrical solemnity which social-documentary TIE can easily fall into (especially if it is polemical), those who want fun above all are unwittingly seeking to trivialise children's theatre. The quasi- mystical word 'magic'—too often used in the same reverent breath as 'Theatre'— belongs no more to theatre for children than for adults, while it remains a generalised concept. The magic of theatrical illusion is as capable of analysis as the magic of a professional illusionist. Like him, to practise the mystery we must first know and be able to control its constituent skills. To achieve communication of the aims of the play or programme, the young members of the audience must be persuaded to identify with it as strongly as possible throughout (even if they are going to be periodically alienated). This has to be done with skilful and responsible manipulation of the primary and secondary theatrical elements outlined above.

Everyone will agree that good theatre for children, with TIE under that umbrella, deserves the best in production techniques, effort, literary craftsmanship and expense (whether it gets them is another matter). Endlessly reworked 'favourite' stories and legends, sagging under the archetypal weight of their clichés, need not constitute most of the subject matter; what counts is not the magic of the content but what is made of it, the underlying motive that gives it its power. To do less in the name of magic is not good children's theatre, nor TIE at all, since it undervalues the children's ability and desire to stretch their understanding and receive new experiences; it patronises them.

What perhaps more than anything defines both the dramatic nature of the programme and its theatrical impact is the *word*—language. The very use of powerfully emotive words, helping to create and sustain the spell of identification, is an educational experi- ence for young children. For some, those who are articulate, and those exposed to articulacy in their lives, it fascinatingly reinforces their dawning understanding of the power and responsibility of words. These children will often play with words unself-consciously and be delighted to find new relationships and effects of language—much of the language of children's games, their jokes and humour, consists of puns, verbal traps, metaphors, and echoisms. For the less articulate, usually just as aware of the power of language, but frightened or humiliated by their own inability to cope with it or control it as well as their fellows can, it can dazzle and excite, free from subsequent rebuke or failure—the fact that they are held enthralled is enough; since there are (unless the teacher is very stupid) no 'tests' afterwards, they will not have to prove by actions that they have understood in detail.

The language, therefore, must be as tight as the characterisation, and in this too the medium has its advantages and its drawbacks. Since many of the programmes are conceived co-operatively by their teams, the aims and structure are worked out first, frequently by a process of improvisation, and the dialogue is left till last. Few teams can afford the luxury of a professional scriptwriter, so the dialogue often falls short of the effects rather glibly implied above in words like 'enthralled', 'spell'. One programme, very imaginatively conceived, had a thrilling story about the Aztec quest for a homeland, emphasising their warlike destiny by contrast with the peaceful traditionalism of the Toltecs they were supplanting.[9] All the dramatic elements were there except the language. The idea of a narrator in the form of a cowardly minor god portrayed with peasant realism and a cockney accent was quite acceptable; it was first of all weakened by two Aztec soldiers who spoke and acted identically to him (rather belying the frequently reiterated assertions about Aztec military omnipotence). The Aztec and Toltec kings were equally banal, but the dignity of their movement and the excitement of the perilous journey to meet the great god Quetzalcoatl maintained the children's interest; when the god appeared, however, and confessed, 'Yeah, well, um, I haven't got much chance if I fight him, have I?' or something just as ungodlike, some of the older children noticed, and commented afterwards that he didn't seem much of a god. Towards the end of the programme the actors fought nobly with their anti-climaxes, but the audience's attention became more and more superficial.

On the other hand, the tighter dialogue of 'The Ballad of Billy Martin' took the amateur company which produced it over a year to evolve, because it was first of all improvised, then scripted, revised, and refined.

Though this frequent looseness, which has sometimes given TIE a bad name among those concerned for the use of language in performance and in schools, is often seen in the scripted work of inexperienced or hurried teams, the greatest danger of it is while working with the children in participatory sequences. Where the children's ideas are being elicited, responded to and used, the context is genuinely improvisation; most such programmes have moments of scripted theatricality built in, but when a child asks a question it must be answered, off the cuff, immediately and in role, in a way that reinforces, not damages, the structure of the ensuing action. Here, often, the teacher in the actor/teacher rears his ugly head, and the characterisation disintegrates into the amorphous generalisation which has been mentioned earlier. *The Happy Land* is the kind of programme particularly prone to this, and characters like the audience-security-figure (usually known as the *link*—in this case, the Chamberlain), the protagonist (the Princess) and the rescuer (the Toymaker) can become almost indistinguishable apart from their costumes as concentration on providing for the children's contributions within the context of the storyline leaves them all exuding the notion:

> 'I am a kind and responsive adult—you can trust me and I will keep you basically safe—but I need your help, so will you—now that's a good idea—what a good idea that is—isn't that a good idea? . . .'

Characters, cornered in participatory improvisation by an idea they had not expected, almost inevitably talk too much as they wrestle simultaneously with the contribution, the situation, and their own role security; in *The Happy Land*, when a child found the doll's head long before the Toymaker was to be mentioned or brought on, the Princess and Chamberlain talked themselves into decreasing circles trying to figure out a way to let the Toymaker, offstage and out of earshot, know. Through the actors' stalling talk the situation may clarify, but while they talk the tension dissipates.

Many teams, especially the more experienced, are well aware of these pitfalls, and avoid them with skill and subtlety, so the picture is not of an unrelieved slide towards a low standard of trite mediocrity. Curiously, the very factors that encourage bad dialogue—the co-operative and many-handed nature of the writing, and the unpredictability of improvisation—can also be the roots of very good dialogue. Language springing from actors' preliminary improvisations needs to be refined into moments of theatre, and it can then be very powerful; originating in an experience that several participants can accept as 'true' (credible and valid for them), it arises straight from dramatic necessity: the words are the right ones, and do not need to be tried out in rehearsal, or against the dramatist's and director's own judgment. They express the drama because the sequence of dramatic thought only exists in them. The right words, but invariably too many of them, and not always the most pungent; the process of refinement is always to be done with a sharp and ruthless knife, as the 'living through' is changed to theatre; the repetitions and self-contradictions have to be pared down or excised, slack phrases must be replaced with accurate ones. The gist is always there, a firm basis, true to the actors' experience. The actor/teacher, too, can avoid the vagaries in participation work by being steeped in his role, saying as little as possible; it is quite feasible, then, to structure each moment theatrically, because what is said is bound to be appropriate.

Any company preparing TIE programmes needs to bear in mind all these dimensions of drama and theatricality. One local education authority drama adviser defines them clearly: 'The work needs proper context, informed preparation with real knowledge of children, good scripts and adequate rehearsal, a top-quality director/leader and a clear programme with aims and objectives clearly thought out.'

Companies who neglect any of these should perhaps note the ominous words of another drama adviser, sympathetic to the principle of TIE: 'These days, whenever I see the words "devised and adapted by the company", I think twice before booking them.'

Chapter Three

Educational aims and claims

'It is possible to use Drama to escape to life or from it' (John Hodgson).[10]

A chapter headed by such a portentous quotation needs to assume a humility often ignored by proponents of new ideas in education as well as by exponents of old ones: namely, that any experience of one or at most a few hours, taken in the context of ten years of formal schooling and a lot more of life's education, can hardly have more than an infinitesimal effect on the total knowledge, personality development, skills, outlook and attitudes of a grown human being (unless the experience is a trauma, about which more will be said later!).

It has often been noted, with sad puzzlement, that those who have been exposed to the purifying and civilising influence of great literature do not act noticeably more purely or in a more civilised way than the totally illiterate. Even granting the questionable assumption about literature, several years of forgiving and being forgiven by one's parents, of kicking and being kicked round school playgrounds, are likely to have vastly more influence on the development of a person's response to a plea for forgiveness than any amount of exposure to *The Tempest*. Education is a process of attrition; the most one can hope for from *The Tempest* is that the balance of outlook might be shifted a fraction (if one is didactically inclined), or at least a microscopic fragment of significant experience might be added to the individual's power of *choice* of action. This is as true of TIE as it is of Shakespeare and all literature, which is not to deny their importance —merely to put into perspective some of the wilder claims made for educational drama and aspersions made against it by those who hail it as an educational panacea, hope to apply it to everything, discount it as irrelevant, fear it as seditious, condemn it as a waste of time, or write chapters like this about its educational aims.

Having said that, and silently prefixing every adjective by 'a little', it is possible to outline the educational functions, both general and specific, which may be served or at least serviced by the twin techniques of presentational and participatory TIE. To begin with, it is fun, or exciting, or at least different. The experience of a TIE programme is usually enjoyed, even if it is a bad one; rarely is it in the children's eyes a total dead loss, though adult observers may be more discriminating or jaundiced. The normal initial response when a travelling company arrives at a school is great excitement from juniors and, in senior schools, a livening of interest expressed with the restrained curiosity of adolescents. There is never any shortage of helpers to unload the van. Thus the actor/teachers start their educational purpose with this great advantage of arresting attention, the first step towards motivation. At its most basic, the van's arrival (or the coach trip to the theatre) means a change from routine. The glamour of strangers looking unusual and doing unusual things is a novelty which particularly appeals to those for whom the norm is unsatisfying, irrelevant, or confusing; those to whom school is interesting and stimulating anyway are no less receptive to this novel glamour. There may occasionally be the odd child, or a class of rebels, who greet the team with hostility, suspecting, quite justifiably from their point of view, that this is another confidence trick that the institution is using to get them to swallow its unacceptable or unpalatable ideas. Even here, the TIE team has the advantage of factors not readily available to the class teacher: the natural motivational forces of drama, theatre and participation. These can reach down and tap desires for education which exist as a natural human need more basic and fundamental than a child's attitude to his schooling.

Drama is a nearly universal activity among adults in tribes from the Aryan Technological to the New Guinea Neolithic. Children's exploratory play acquires some measure of dramatic content very early—my own daughter was three when one morning, mildly irritated by my nagging, she picked up an L-shaped toast crust and unhesitatingly shot me dead with it. In the case of my own children, and no doubt most other people's, drama developed more or less simultaneously with the realisation of other people's value as play partners. The level of dramatic content increases as children become older; having established an understanding of their own self-interest, they start to explore group relationships and interests, in complex games of good versus bad, or the formation, interaction and manipulation of gangs and cliques. Often the dramatic content is ritualised, usually into competitive sports by boys and intricate pattern games by girls.

The ability to identify with characters presented never dwindles or leaves us; we all continue to enjoy the educational opportunity to explore through the vicissitudes of our hero our attitudes to crises of love, courage, loyalty, fear, and our understanding of the appropriateness of role behaviour, or, at the simple, satisfying level of soap opera, to have our preconceptions comfortably confirmed. (Educational, did I say? Well, it is perfectly valid to argue, with a static view of society, that if those preconceptions are socially acceptable, then it is in the interests both of the society and the individual, and therefore educational, to reinforce them. Of this too, more later.)

It does not take Chinese proverbial platitudes to tell us that in education seeing is better than hearing, and doing better than seeing. Whether the audience takes part actively in a TIE programme, or whether the children just sit and watch a presentation, they are understanding by doing rather than seeing. They do not dispassionately watch, as they might a chemical experiment or a vaulting demonstration; their emotions are actively engaged, willing and desiring and responding to the tensions and humours of the action.

Two more forces are at work together, creating in the child a natural organic educational motive: those of recognition and curiosity. In all except very deprived children the desire to know more, to receive new impulses and experiences, is very strong, so the alien world brought by the strangers is bound to be at least initially exciting. (I have had pointed out to me educationally subnormal children from inadequate backgrounds who do not know how to play together, and have to be taught the rudiments of social and dramatic play even in the playground.) Frustration and tedium quickly set in if that world is so alien as to be incomprehensible, so the team always needs to start from where the child *is*. The child needs the immediate satisfaction of recognising that the situation in some way ties in with his perception and knowledge of his world. First, this is necessary to engender security, particularly in a young child struggling to develop a coherent picture of the experiences and impressions pouring in on him, a picture which will help him to know how to respond to them. If he is suddenly presented with an experience which completely disorients him, particularly if it is aimed powerfully at the emotions and is spectacular, he will not be able to cope, and will usually respond in one of three ways, either by bursting into tears and rushing for his teacher in fear, or by inattention and fidgets, or by a noisy over-reaction, showing his displeasure by negatively 'sending-up' the performance because to him it is 'silly'. It is just as important with older children to remember that relevance, like beauty, is in the eye of the beholder, and that the content, however vitally important to the actors or writer, will only have impact on the children if it can strike a chord of recognition. If they can understand where the action starts from, and be aware, throughout, of why it is progressing, they will follow it with rapt attention for a very long time. Older children, not having the retreat of bursting into tears available to them, invariably take refuge from a programme that is not relevant by the other two methods.

These gloomily negative observations are untypical, though. Most programmes gain and keep their audience's attention for most of the time, and provide a satisfying experience. Where they fail it is because they have ignored or mishandled basic positive motive forces. It is not too difficult, if you know something about the interests of an age-range of children, to find a suitable model or hero to identify with, a situation and storyline both recognisable and excitingly unpredictable, and (perhaps most important) a satisfying conclusion (not necessarily the same thing as a happy ending). The children expect this, from their previous experience with stories, television and their own play; it may well be an open ending, but it must be clearly provided and it must represent the sum of their understanding of the process of the play (story and theme). Then it will be satisfying.

Each programme will also generate its own motivation for attention, according to its educational aim. It may be the sense of success generated by overcoming a problem almost, but not quite, too difficult to solve; it might be the relief and recognition of seeing dangerous emotions externalised; sometimes it is the pleasure of having ideas or facts clarified which were hazily understood.

Though motivation and deep involvement do not in themselves constitute learning, they are necessary conditions for the kind of learning which theatre and drama in education offer, replacing the carrot and the whip, the house point and the cane. The concept that motivation in schooling, like the discipline referred to in Chapter 2, should be from within, is one of the changing concepts that makes schooling more difficult and rewarding, teachers more frustrated and dedicated, a child's experience of school more confusing and varied, and theatre in education possible at all.

This sense of change often expresses itself in schools, particularly in secondary schools, as a problem of polarisation. In its most extreme form there is a very clear politico-philosophical dichotomy expressed in the different and conflicting policies pursued by head teachers, heads of departments or faculties, and individual teachers, within the same large school. It is doubly confusing because many, seeing both sides, try to run with the hare and hunt with the hounds. The conflict is often expressed in superficially simple, and therefore misleading, terminology of conservatism versus progress: 'Schooling versus education for autonomy' (Illich and Reimer),[11] 'Banking and skills developing education must be replaced by the praxis... Knowledge consists of invention and re-invention' (Freire).[12]

Fundamentally, apparently, it all depends on your view of society. If you believe that social reality is something objective into which we have been born, and which continues to exist because its values are passed on; that there are such things as right and wrong; that a sense of these has to be inculcated, drawn forth, or perpetuated; that stability and authority are essential parts of a healthy society; and that our society is *basically* healthy; then to you education will be of a static and didactic nature. It will pass on the skills and attitudes reflected in the society itself, the values important to it, and the codes, modes and mores of behaviour acceptable to it. It will place emphasis on developing an individual's sense of responsibility to the society and teach a respect for tradition and for law and order, along with the value of conformity.

If on the other hand you think that social reality only exists in people's perception of it; that each individual's perception will be in subtle emphases and tinges differing according to his upbringing, the status and positions he holds in society; that right and wrong are relative terms, definable only within a particular social context; and that the perceptions, shared and individual (and thus the social reality, too) are capable of alteration, necessary alteration; then your education will be of a dynamic and open-ended nature. It will attempt to develop powers of critical judgment, a sense of personal responsibility, where the individual is able to assess a situation, develop his own personal response rather than rely on a traditional pattern of behaviour, and reflectively assess the consequences in the context of the social interaction as he understands it, instead of merely reacting to it. You will try to develop the self-control and systematic, imaginative thinking which allow self-directed and co-operative learning, instead of authoritative teaching and competitive assimilation.

Traditionally the English educational system, like any other, has been built up to serve the first of these ends. Now the system, more sensitive than many rigid and centralised educational systems in other countries, mirrors the struggles between conservatism, evolution and revolution which characterise the society that it serves.

In practice, the conflicts between head and head, head and assistant, or assistant and assistant are mostly expressed in personal clashes and animosities based on frustration. A teacher concerned with developing a sense of academic responsibility in her pupils as she endeavours to give them sufficient information and background understanding to pass their O-level French is understandably exasperated when her children arrive noisy and excited from Drama, and the lesson is accompanied by periodic bumps, howls, hammerings and roars of laughter from the Art studio above, as well as the continuous, muffled, but penetrating chatter of an English project next door—and when half her students are away on a field trip anyway. It is sometimes understandably malicious comfort to know that the English teacher is equally exasperated with the way the children exploit the free atmosphere of his lessons to work off the energy repressed during the inhibiting rigour of their French lesson, or the way most of them prefer unthinking dependence on his word to the moral pressures of a self-directed learning which much of their previous schooling has either left them unprepared for or actively discouraged.

The result is often a perpetual irritation, a succession of staffroom rows, or at worst resignation, as teachers either take refuge in an extreme which at least presents a picture of their roles in life that offers security and self-esteem ('Teaching is revolutionary —we must sweep away the dross of outdated ideas', or 'I'm just old-fashioned; I want to uphold values and standards'), or have a foot in both camps and suffer accordingly, as they endeavour to develop a teaching technique which faces both ways at once, saying simultaneously to the pupils, 'I am part of the system; this institution of schooling transmits valuable standards and I am committed to upholding those standards', and 'I believe in progress and enlightenment; you must learn to think for yourselves, develop your own skills of discrimination and question everything, including what I say.'

One of the truisms—nonetheless true—of developing a good working relationship with a class is that the teacher must present a clear persona to the children, so that the boundaries of acceptable response are clearly defined and consistently upheld; it is not surprising that many teachers with this equivocal attitude to their own function, especially inexperienced ones, succeed merely in baffling the children as they appear to offer a free and fraternal relationship, then as soon as a child accidentally oversteps the unmarked boundary, or deliberately sets out to test the genuineness of this suspicious bonhomie, they nervously retreat behind the battlements of the institution with its defensive armoury of routines and sanctions, authority and punishment. Where the teachers are able to outline clear patterns of behaviour, the children are still prone to disorientation as, in the secondary school's fragmented curricula, they reel from class to class, from free-thinking mathematician to authoritarian Humanities specialist, and liable, if they commit a venial sin on the way, to be faced with any one of ten quite different responses, depending on which member of staff saw them do it.

Put negatively, this sounds massively condemnatory. There is another positive side. The interplay of these two powerful philosophies creates an atmosphere of ready evolution, of change within the system. Many teachers are radically self-critical; the dictatorial powers of ossified examination and matriculation syllabuses are gradually becoming eroded and replaced by school-based assessments on broader fronts, and the development of independent curricula; 'non-academic' subjects like educational drama and social studies are gaining respectability and establishment on timetables from infant school upwards. The almost total autonomy of many head teachers, and the autonomy that some of them grant to individual teachers and departments, has enabled many ordinary teachers to plunge into mixed-ability teaching, pastoral counselling, integrated studies and days, child-centred learning and Mode 3 assessment without fear of drowning, because there are still safety lines to cling on to, the lines of traditional educational practice. Children still need to read and write, exhibit appropriate certificates to employers and college registrars, and the nature of the institution is still recognisably the same—twelve years or so, nine to four, adults (organisers and distributors) differentiated from children (consumers) and so on.

Good teachers develop their own techniques to stay afloat, techniques which in time become sufficiently clear formulations for younger or less proficient colleagues to cling to. Sometimes these methods are developed from forces within combining with those outside, as in the Nuffield projects, the modern mathematics movement, or Schools Council projects like the *Breakthrough to Literacy* scheme, and as in theatre in education, which very much reflects the clash of the forces which created it. Like many subject disciplines and teaching techniques, TIE was born in and of the flux, and the majority of companies are strongly committed to the idea of 'progressive', open-ended education, and propagate its ideals with missionary zeal. Others, more committed still, have opted out of the system, and either just work outside school hours and premises, or use the schools' own time to discredit the institution and the establishment they believe it stands for.

This is perhaps a pity, because, looked at from another angle, this whole vaguely apocalyptic vision of a struggle between Good and Evil (or evil and good, depending which side you are on!) is an over-simplification. It is equally possible, without ignoring the political considerations, to consider the whole educational area as another continuum, with all the processes of instillation, distillation, inculcation, inspiration, creative development, indoctrination, nurture and all the other misleading metaphors as points on the continuum.

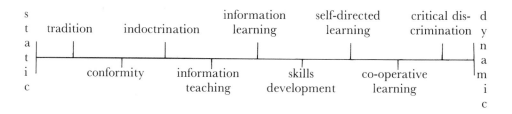

You do not have to agree with the exact order or comprehensiveness of this continuum to see that differences in the approaches of teachers can be considered of degree, not kind. To take an example, to teach an understanding of the dictates, rules and laws of society is not incompatible with attempting to develop an awareness of the advantages and disadvantages; in fact it is a prerequisite for developing an understanding of both social and individual responsibility, of the relationship between these two factors, and of the consequences of action. This can be of practical value when considering the particular areas of education. All teachers would acknowledge their responsibility towards cognitive, affective, imaginative and social development, to use an unoriginal and fashionable categorisation. (The last two, though they are perhaps composed of the elements of the first, need separate emphasis as different fusions of those elements.) The emphasis on each is what is different.

Theatre in education has its contribution to make towards all these four areas, and the specific disciplines which they spawn.

General areas of development

Cognitive

It is not fortuitous that developing more or less simultaneously with TIE, though at first independently, have been simulation teaching techniques. Games of the kind that used to be played respectably at Christmas (like *Monopoly*), or surreptitiously under the desks during boring lessons (like *Battleships*), are increasingly being used as key activities in the classroom, particularly in secondary schools and colleges. A teacher of geography who wishes to explain the possibilities and problems of North Sea oil exploration produces a map of the North Sea divided into squares, a set of dice, toy money and a pack of cards representing control factors. The children form companies, plan and bargain; to succeed they have to learn to recognise the opportunities available and the obstacles ahead, and to use the tools they have been given to take the opportunities and master the obstacles.[13]

Most of the early development of teaching games took place in America, and the emphasis was on competition, each child struggling to win against the rest. In England, the trend has been to use the problem itself as the competitive challenge. Some links with TIE begin to appear: the children form groups endowed with particular interests in a problematic situation. Sometimes they race parallel (perhaps to discover who will be successful in acquiring the development franchise—the 'industrialists', the 'conservationists', or the 'private builders'); sometimes in direct opposition ('Trade Unions' versus 'Management', or 'Napoleon' versus 'Wellington'); sometimes each group works independently to solve the problem and then the various solutions are compared. When they are playing a game of this kind the children are really role-playing, identifying with a symbolic set of interests and often acquiring a very strong, even fierce, empathy with their role. A problem of dramatic conflict is presented, the children are invited to participate by identifying with protagonists in the conflict, and working in a structured situation to resolve the conflict.

A key link with TIE is in the word 'play'. As already implied, both educational drama and these simulation games have their roots in the function that children's play seems to have of ritualising forms of exploration—in both, the process is enjoyable if it is challenging, clear, and progressing towards some kind of satisfying conclusion.

An even more important link is the concept central to the philosophy of teaching by simulation: that of models. In preparing a simulation game the teacher extracts from what he knows about the subject he wishes to teach those elements which are the most important, the underlying ideas, or at least those he feels his pupils can cope with. (He must himself have clear understanding of it and a stable attitude towards it.) From the mass of factual detail surrounding these fundamentals he selects only what is essential both to understand how the concept relates to the factual reality as the child sees it, and to make the concept dynamic, so that the pupil can see the forces of action and consequence, cause and effect, at work.

'Models can be viewed as selective approximations which by the elimination of incidental detail allow some fundamental relevant or interesting aspects of the real world to appear in some generalised form' (R. J. Chorley and P. Huggett).[14]

'In practice, models are chains of ideas linked together and observed at work: skeletons which can be made to dance at the command of the observer' (R. Walford).[13]

'Model', then, is another name for what in the world of drama has long been known as a 'theme'; the 'selective approximation' is exactly what writers of plays and presenters of TIE programmes are making; when it can be made to 'dance at the command of the observer', we call it integral participation.

TIE as a form or at least an extension of simulation becomes clearer still when we consider another kind of simulation technique, enormously popular at all levels of teaching, in any situation where an understanding of aspects of human interaction is desired: the case study. In this form of teaching, students are presented with a fictitious context in which characters are shown to be in conflict; just sufficient background detail is given to provide an understanding of the problem's causes, and the student is often first asked a 'negative' comprehension question: 'How did this situation arise?' In addition he is usually also asked, 'What can be done to solve the problem—break the deadlock—create better conditions?' If the students cannot be expected to have enough information in their own knowledge, then clues are implanted, often ambiguously, to generate a fruitful discussion of alternatives. In a recent experiment some material about a social worker's casebook was developed as a case study lesson *and* as a TIE programme, in both forms for fifteen-year-olds in Social Studies classes. The material adapted perfectly well to both media of presentation, and the response to it from the pupils, though different in some ways, was in essence similar.[15]

Bringing back to memory that useful old Chinese platitude, 'I hear: I forget—I see: I remember—I do: I understand', we recognise that the advantages to cognitive learning, then, of TIE are likely to be those of any use of models, whether made of plaster-of-paris and polystyrene ('I see: I remember'), chequered maps and fictitious companies ('I do: I understand'), or actors in character and costume (both). One may hope that both the visual content and their personal involvement will help pupils understand by making them want to do so, and showing them the processes of geography, family life, politics, or whatever, laid bare to their working essentials. Children—and adults—often despair of trying to understand fundamental issues because of the jungle of facts, statistics, and related subjects which needs to be struggled through first. This the teacher or programme compiler can hack away, leaving a clearer path. The student should be left with a structured understanding of basic processes rather than a knowledge of facts which, unrelated, may be valueless; this structuring should in turn help both memory and the transfer of understanding to related processes.

It is not surprising, therefore, that TIE companies have seized on simulation techniques as part of their repertoire. Programmes often include games and case studies in their follow-up suggestions, and even within the programme. One company has gone so far as to use the pupils as the 'pieces' in a giant board game. It would not be fair, however, to suggest that teams have parasitically fastened on to others' ideas. That there has been a natural progression based on the mutual use of models can be seen in this description of the Coventry Belgrade TIE's 1970 programme *The Emergent Africa Game*.

The Emergent Africa Game   Autumn Term 1970
For pupils 14–18

The success of the Stoke Hill Wood project [a senior programme involving the use of simulation of a fictitious community] led us to plan further secondary work in which the audience play roles in a simulated situation. At this time a drama specialist from Ghana . . . was seconded to us. Then we came across *States of Emergency* by Dennis Guerrier and Joan Richards, which was described as a 'programmed novel'. The authors had taken the problems of emergent African states and invented a composite state, 'Lakoto'. At each stage the reader was invited to choose what he would do as prime minister. Here was the basic research for a drama game, and we used the characters and situations of *States of Emergency* as the basis for audience participation.

The project toured schools playing to 4th, 5th and 6th forms. The audience was between 100 and 120, and the session lasted a half day. The audience are sitting in a horseshoe round a playing area backed by a rear projection screen. The stage manager introduces herself. 'Could you govern a country? We invite you to find out.' Independence Day. The Princess presents a parliamentary mace, the symbol of democracy from the Mother of Parliaments at Westminster to the Prime Minister, Okobo. The Union Jack is replaced by the new flag of Lakoto.

What are this country's chances? The stage manager summons a British reporter, Clare Furnival, who outlines Lakoto's geography and history. It is composed of two tribes, the majority peasant tribe, the Cantarbis, and the merchant class, the Mokans.

Clare interviews the Prime Minister Okobo, a democrat educated in England, founder of the Centre Party. She meets Karome, leader of the Cantarbi Nationalists, at a street demonstration. Lakoto's problems have only just begun.

First cabinet meeting. What is to be the new nation's first priority? A Mokan merchant makes out a case for using their financial resources for recruiting *experts from abroad* to start developing agriculture and industry at once. Karome disagrees violently, the priority should be the peasants in the shanty town. They need a *welfare service* to cope with the problems of unemployment. Another Cantarbi argues that the priority should be *education*, basic literacy, otherwise the people will never break away from ignorance and superstition. Already the cabinet is split.

The stage manager intervenes and turns to the audience. Which course of action would you support if you were Prime Minister?

The audience divides into groups of 12 to 15. The actors act as discussion leaders. With some pupils the issues have to be explained again. But perhaps someone supports one alternative and stimulates an argument. After ten minutes the actors return from the audience and the stage manager takes a vote to see which course of action they approve of. . . . What does Okobo support? He outlines the arguments as he sees them. He needs to find a role as mediator and a priority to unite his people. He chooses *education*. Time will tell if he has chosen wisely.

Clare visits a hydro-electric scheme and the audience share in a subsequent cabinet

Which course of action? (*The Emergent Africa Game*)

decision about the use of basic resources. Then we meet General Nashur. He believes in strong government. If the democratic cabinet system fails to govern effectively, it will be the duty of the army to restore law and order and take control. The sole member of the Lakoto Secret Service reports this to Okobo. Nashur has done nothing openly treasonable, but we know his opinions. The M.I.5 agent recommends that General Nashur should be the victim of a convenient accident. The stage manager intervenes; Okobo can condone political assassination to safeguard democracy, or wait for Nashur to move and arrest him for treason, or send him on a diplomatic mission abroad.

The audience discuss in groups the advisability and morality of this issue. Most pupils vote for assassination. Their response may have been superficial, or they may be facing the reality of the situation with a positive act. Okobo cannot accept this. He sends Nashur abroad. Is he weak or honourable? Time will tell if he is right.

Clare hears of riots in a border town, Benallahi. She drives there to investigate. A series of projected slides show us the type of town and the riots. Clare is accidentally killed. We have lost our guide and must go there ourselves.

The audience each take a scarf which is either red or green from the back of their seat, divide into two groups and move to separate working spaces. Two parallel drama sessions enable the students to take on the roles of the Cantarbi and Mokan rioters in a town where the better jobs are held by the Mokans. Because of the riots the factories close and there is no work. Both groups in their roles converge on the playing area which becomes the market place. Karome arrives from the capital. The audience are now involved in an improvisation. Karome asks for details of their troubles and puts forward his solution—partition, Cantarbs to the East, Mokans to the West. The people may greet this with approval or reject it.

He is challenged by a man in a combat jacket. 'The root of your problems is not tribal hate but poverty. Forget your tribes, combine together, let us take over the factories and run them ourselves.' The pupils know enough to recognise the alternatives, though they may not be able to name them. They may not previously have taken any interest in politics. Now they are exploring partition and Castro-style socialism, but not theoretically, they are on their feet in a drama situation. The man in the combat jacket is Ngami. He appeals for all those who will reject tribalism and join the workers' combine to throw down their tribal scarves. Red and green scarves pile up. Some pupils won't join, they are suspicious of his motives, they don't trust him.

The stage manager stops the action. He gives Ngami a sten gun. Will he use force to maintain a popular movement? Ngami pauses. Some of his supporters are unsure. He decides—Yes. 'Those who resist us will be executed.' Ngami stands for revolutionary action, not the slow processes of democracy. The audience return to their seats discussing Ngami's decision. They revert to being an audience.

The actors play out the results of the rebellion. Okobo must decide whether to crush a popular movement caused by discontent over social conditions. Was he right to put education as his first priority? While he hesitates, General Nashur acts. The M.I.5 agent assassinates him (unknown to Okobo) in order to prevent a military coup. Was Okobo right to refuse this plan of action earlier? A neighbouring state, Mokoran, plans to annex part of Lakoto under the pretext of protecting her investments. Okobo appeals successfully to the United Nations and achieves a breathing space.

The stage manager interrupts the action. Three men have the ability to govern Lakoto: Okobo the democrat, Ngami the Marxist revolutionary, Karome the partitionist. Which one is right?

This programme worked successfully for senior pupils of all ability levels. Different issues emerged each time it was played.[16]

This programme shows how the TIE team can play its part in modernising educational practice by helping teachers to develop an approach that is more concerned with concepts than content; simulations involve the students not in learning about a topic but in realising it in all senses. The idea is, of course, fraught with danger: the very words 'structuring' and 'selection' of material sound the note of alarm, or ought to. The spectres of dogma, of presenting answers instead of questions and points of ideological view as truths, of the closed-up or heavily slanted ending, lurk just as menacingly as in overtly didactic traditional teaching.

Affective
'What is the nature and function of drama when it operates at the highest level of achievement? When it is composed of those elements common to both children's play

and theatre, when the aims are to help children to learn about those feelings, attitudes and preconceptions which before the drama was experienced were too implicit for them to be aware of' (Gavin Bolton).[10]

In recent years an awareness has grown among educationists of areas of personality other than the intellectual or cognitive which perhaps need aid towards development. Perhaps emotional maturity is not automatically acquired along with extra inches. Heads and teachers recognise, often grudgingly or guiltily, that there is a need for what they vaguely call 'education of the emotions' or 'affective development'. Previously almost totally ignored by the educational system, except when they got in the way of the intellectual processing and had to be repressed, the emotional forces which guide, stimulate and form the background to every person's self-image, his very reasonableness and his relationships with others, need development and control. Yes, but how? Each child's emotions are different, his responses individual and unpredictable.

Up to a point this is true; but the emotions we feel are shared in some degree by everybody, and the first step towards guiding and controlling one's emotions is to accept their presence and understand them. There seems to be approximately the same homogeneity in children's natural emotional development as their intellectual (the two are of course inseparably linked, in all except the way we treat them in schools) which can provide us with clues as clear as Piaget's. For instance, young infants of the same age are all ego-centred, and respond in a similar way to cues signalling rejection, love, protection, the difference between me-things and them-things, and so on; they are usually frightened of the same bogeys and need the same security symbols. An outward-looking and inquisitive eight-year-old, and an adolescent rediscovering his identity because the reactions of the person he thought he was have changed, each needs his own set of cues, though many of the emotions elicited are the same. Consider these statements: each of them will normally produce a strong response of fear and guilt at one of these ages, and little effect at all at the others:

'The witch is waiting for you.'
'We don't like you, you're wet.'
'That's a nasty, dirty habit.'

Educational drama usually gets its lodgment on the timetable as a possible answer to that perplexing question, 'Yes, but how?' Passions roused and sated, and the dramatic impulse of identification in a commitment of emotion, are traditionally the staple fare of drama. Even if your Brechtian aim is to alienate the intellectual response from the emotional empathy, it is necessary to find out the strength of that empathy, how you can trap it, and what you are going to do with it to keep it out of the way.

Through drama, an individual may fleetingly fulfil thwarted desires by vicariously sharing them with the hero or acting them out in a risk-free environment. Drama may go further in opening up taboos or attempting therapy, though the whole issue of the actor/teacher's responsibilities, to the child, his parents, the school, needs fuller discussion elsewhere (see Chapter 7, pages 133–45). Some years ago a programme entitled *She's leaving Home* was played to audiences of fourteen-year-olds, many of whom have powerfully ambivalent feelings towards their home environment, with conflicting desires for independence and dependence. The programme presented a sympathetic portrait of a girl who was unhappy at home; it was sympathetic too towards her family. The gradual breakdown of the family bond was depicted, each party's share in the responsibility shown quite honestly, and the play ended with the girl hesitating as she was about to walk out of the door for the last time. Did she, or didn't she?* In discussion afterwards some of the students thought she would leave, some thought not. More important, they all agreed that they had learned things that they could apply to their own home circumstances; they asserted, some quite forcibly, that their behaviour and attitude to their family environment would change. (Whether it did or not, and if so to what degree and for how many months, hours, or minutes, nobody knows, of course!) Several felt that the programme crystallised their emotional reactions in a way which had not been possible before—emotions which, for varying personal reasons, few of them had been able to discuss with parents, or with friends, or even admit to themselves. By bringing out into the open repressed feelings, externalising them, they thought it had assisted them to come to terms with such feelings.

In all probability this is considerably overstating the case. There is no doubt, though, that dramatic symbols may have a powerful effect on the spectator. An infant programme,[17] described later (see Appendix, pages 146–58), contained a mysterious character called The Pest, who could be heard but not seen, and who flew round playing mischievous tricks. The children latched on to this character with fascination; one child insisted, in tears, on the way back to the classroom, that The Pest had bitten him, and for days, even weeks afterwards any small accident that could not be immediately explained was attributed to The Pest.

One of the functions of the drama teacher, and also of the TIE team, is to construct contexts where children may explore their emotions judged only by themselves, or where they can reveal their emotions experimentally but retreat if they are hurt. 'It wasn't me doing that, it's just the play.' In this kind of situation a cushioned reality enters the drama, a poignant example of which occurred in a recent drama lesson.

Twelve-year-olds were exploring, in the situation of a 'mental hospital', what madness is. In setting up the programme, the teacher had concentrated on the nature of obsession. To start some interaction in this rather solitary session, the teacher, role-playing a 'doctor', asked for volunteers to come forward to be questioned, publicly, by three 'medical students'. The second volunteer, Mary, was a girl of slightly restricted growth, very much an isolate in the class, who had developed a superficially cocksure imperviousness to the frequent snubs, bullying and taunts she received, often about her size; wisely, she had learnt not to rise to the bait. Slightly tongue in cheek, the 'students' started the questioning.

'What's your name?'
'Mary.' (Most of the 'patients' had changed theirs.)
'Tell us something about yourself, Mary.'
'I'm a giant.'

At this the 'students', forgetting their roles, started to snigger. Mary whirled round on them.

'Yes, I am, I'm a giant; I'm ten feet tall, taller than any of you.'

The words were not shouted, but spoken with such demonic intensity that every smirk vanished instantly, and a breathless silence followed. No more was said then or later, but according to Mary the taunts about her size stopped for a while.

This was not, as it happened, a TIE programme, but where children are given freedom to express themselves in role this kind of tentative self-projection is not uncommon, though it is more difficult for the actor/teacher, who does not know the individual children well, to recognise it.

In the freedom of identification or role-play a child can experience the thrill of heroism, the excitement of vicarious fear, the problems of leadership. In one programme, the children have to elect their leader. He or she is given a number of tasks, fairly simply accomplished with the actor/characters' help, to build up confidence, then in consultation with other members of his 'army of justice' he has to make a decision which will have consequences for all of them. The army gives him as much advice as he can get by his powers of leadership, but the decision is his, and on it rests the way the play will go.[18]

Imaginative

All teachers in primary schools, and in 'arts' subjects in the secondary school, have long acknowledged or at least paid lip service to the importance of developing imagination and creativity, though few like being asked to define them. So most of us do our best to cater for them in our syllabuses, without being any too sure what they are. Words like 'intuition' and 'inspiration' (lateral or divergent thinking, to replace the mystical overtones with quasi-scientific ones) have recently become respectable among scientists, social scientists and mathematicians, as foresight once again becomes fashionable and logical virtuosity frequently and obviously does not bring its own reward.

On the simplest level, theatre in education can provide a marvellous stimulus for the imaginations of children, by enlarging the range of the possible, and helping them perceive 'The wholeness of nature, and one's individual identity within and related to it' (Mary Dilworth).[19] On the first count, though TIE must start from where the children are, it does not have to stop there—and must not, without presenting a new horizon, a new angle or a new view of the known. Using the imaginative projection that theatricality provides, anchored firmly in a child's understanding of what is, anything can be made to seem real.

For younger children there is the well-used stimulus of exploring the unknown, fantasy lands where any character may appear, anything happen. Apart from the operative side of fantasy (dealt with later), children enjoy it most if it has a logical explanation —the logic need not be mundane logic, but children will want to know why giant three-eared pink bunnies are going against common sense by trying to eat the hero, or why the magic spell to make the fat man's banana tree grow resides only with the crab at the bottom of the sea.

Fantasy itself does not necessarily stretch the imagination; it may betray its educational function in two ways. First, if it is too random, too dissociated from the familiar, the imagination may not bother to chase the meaning. So an infant school audience was at first amused by a seven-foot tall character in baggy tennis shorts, clowns' long shoes and a funny hat, hitting a wobbly tennis ball badly—so far, so consistent. When he was joined by Minnie the Minx, a bright green comedy Sherlock Holmes (surely characters from the fantasies of an older range of children anyway), and a talking dog, in a feeble but very complex story of fiendish intrigues and verbal agility, the children first sat in open-mouthed bemusement, then remembered the hardness of the floor on their bottoms. The costumes were marvellous, the play incomprehensible.†

The great and lasting fantasies of children's story-telling have lasted because behind the fantasy lie powerful symbols; there is a troll under every child's bridge to be exorcised by wit and dexterity, while tales like the terrifying *Yallery-Brown* help him to adjust to the fact, obvious enough to his observation, that some will never be exorcised. The ferocious endings of Grimm, and folk tales the world over, mirror the child's own urges to destroy, and help him to exorcise them because it's only a story, and mummy's still there.

Secondly, by the time most children are exposed to TIE, or to any form of theatre, they have been steeped in these stories for some while at the hands of parents, other adults, older brothers and sisters, television and their peers. If there is to be a fantasy element, it should add to the child's stock of archetypes, or present a type in a new and usable way, otherwise the archetypes just become boring stereotypes. Too often the fantasy offered is merely a pale imitation of a symbol with which the child is already totally familiar. (When you've seen one magic forest, you've seen them all. That need not be true, but often seems so.)

As children grow older, the fantasy must turn to fiction, and the imaginative transport becomes less than satisfying if it is merely to far off lands; people's minds are more exciting territory, motives more interesting than actions. How did Florence Nightingale feel when she arrived at Scutari? That dirty old tramp you are looking at, that could be you. Being schizophrenic feels—like this. These are interior landscapes; in externals, too, the older child wants to know why things work, not merely see that they do. In their small way, educational drama and TIE seek to enlarge children's ability to project sympathetically into the minds and motives of others, to give new understanding of why people have behaved so, and still do. Remembering the caveat with which this chapter began, this claim is not pretentious; we do not expect to turn our audiences into humanitarian paragons, merely, briefly, to offer them a new angle. For example, many children have extreme preconceptions about gypsy life; depending on the input from their parents, travelling people are likely to be pigeonholed either as 'the dark-eyed gypsy rovers, oh', or 'them thieving dids down the by-pass'.

After an hour spent identifying with the brave/cunning/downtrodden/humorous/dirty/ respectable/intelligent/clumsy/gormless/articulate/inarticulate son of a brave/cunning/ down-trodden/humorous/dirty/respectable/intelligent/clumsy/gormless/articulate/in-articulate tinker or Romany family, at least the children have a measure of choice. They can ignore their hour and stick to their preconception; they can add to it an acceptance of a possible alternative ('Yes, well, you might get one or two like that'); they can modify their preconception to the degree that they are able to make the imaginative transfer from the fictional story to the real-life possibility—the degree, in fact, to which the fiction works; they can throw away the preconception and want to find out what gypsy life is like; or they can swallow the programme whole, and imagine gypsy life is like what they have seen. More than that is unlikely, though it is possible to argue (and the programme may have been explicitly aimed at this rather highflown ambition) that a significant fragment may be added to the children's understanding of minorities or the rejected.

An imaginative function of TIE may be to show the familiar in a new light, to show unexpected connections and possibilities. Junior school audiences of one pro-gramme were invited to join a glamorous sea-voyage of exploration, searching for riches; towards the end, they were suddenly made to realise in a clever *coup de théâtre* that they were on a slaving expedition.²⁰ In another, the pressures of contemporary living on a young married couple were wryly acted out as an incompetent tight-rope act, the husband's nervous breakdown represented by his fall from the wire.²¹ In this way the metaphor is made concrete and comprehensible. Similarly, in *The Ballad of Billy Martin*, the Warden's tired old aphorism, 'What you lose on the swings, Billy, you gain on the roundabouts', suddenly springs to life in front of him, the tawdry glamour grotesquely mirroring Billy's youthful hopes, and the raucous but ultimately disappoint-ing claims of the fairground barkers echoing the specious choices he is faced with.

As an extension of this, theatre can provide unexpected conclusions, and show that the obvious is not the only. Any programme which finishes up satisfying immediate expectations and reinforcing perspectives that already existed belongs to the realm of soap opera, not education. In participation work, particularly, the opportunity to stretch the children's imaginations is enormous. When the children are asked to find solutions, the actor need not, and usually should not, accept the easiest. How can the rescuers get past the ever-vigilant castle gatekeeper? The children always immediately suggest bribery and pull out a convenient bundle of pretend banknotes. The gatekeeper, however, proves incorruptible, and throws their money into the moat, now more suspicious of them than ever. So imaginations really have to get to work, and an ingenious plan gradually evolves, with diversionary manoeuvres and complicated alibis.[18]

Social

As a general heading this is perhaps misleading, for it covers two processes—first, that of socialisation, which is part of the total personality development of each individual, fostered or adopted over the years with differing degrees of success, along with other related skills, such as the ability to empathise, to project an identification, to listen and converse reciprocally; and secondly, the largely cognitive skill of discovering and learning about how social processes work.

One of the most really significant changes in practice in schools in recent years has been the swing from solitary and competitive learning to co-operative and corporate activity, on the principle that the interaction of peer groups is a useful aid to the teaching situation (or that two heads are better than one). There is, of course, more to it than that. It is belatedly, and by no means universally, coming home to teachers that for most people the greater part of life is not directly combative, the subtle antagonisms and tactical battles of everyday life being far too elusive and delicate for the simple competitiveness traditionally encouraged in schools to be of any assistance. At work, for instance, though it is obviously necessary sometimes to assert oneself aggressively and completely when trying to raise one's status, establish boundaries, maintain one's self-esteem, or fight for beliefs or profit, much work-time is taken up with sharing and getting on with others, at work bench, in shops and offices, whether manager or managed. Besides, work is a slowly but steadily shrinking minority time activity. Our educational system is conspicuously less successful at developing skills of co-operative work-sharing, stable family life and well-regulated social interaction than, say, the

Kalahari Bushman's. In the past, by concentrating on developing the concept of an authority figure, teaching, incontrovertibly, a number of pupils isolated from each other both by the teacher-towards-class structure and the emphasis on comparative value judgment, the apparatus of marks, exams and rewards, status and streaming, the whole system has mediated against socialisation instead of encouraging it.

Teachers are now becoming aware of this, even finding virtues in necessity; when faced with a mixed ability class for the first time, a teacher is bound to wonder how he can 'aim his material' at thirty different targets at the same time. (That there are thirty different targets has always been true anyway, but they have often gone unrecognised in the most rigorously streamed classes.) If the teacher is lucky, he recognises that if the material is worth 'aiming' then it is worth offering, to be drawn on at whatever level each child can manage. He may realise that to some extent the children will have to teach each other. If he gets so far, he is on the edge of breaking through to the realisation of what a marvellous teaching resource he has been wasting all those years; speaking each other's language, the children often know the words to make the concepts stick better than the teachers, and having to express a half-formed idea in order to explain it to someone more ignorant than oneself is the ideal way to clarify it in one's own mind. This is not lazy teaching, but a positive move; children, given half a chance, are very supportive of each other, and like to be given the opportunity to show it, which helps solve that problem of motivation which has raised its head again. Basing their security on the fact that when they thrust their material at pupils, many children spent a lot of time trying to reject it, some teachers are worried that if they offer their goods with a degree of volition, the children will sit back. To the teachers' surprise, when they try it, children seem to work no more lazily than before, and the battle is virtually won in primary schools (it still rages in earnest in the secondary school). Class projects, children working in pairs and groups, wandering about the school, the teacher happily relegated from his dais, are now normal sights as children learn to solve problems and master skills by working together, finding out and learning to utilise or cope with their relative strengths and weaknesses.

Educational drama, whether as a subject in itself or as a technique, can help this process by further changing the social conditions of the learning situation. By role-playing, the teacher can free a range of reactions in the children, normally inhibited by their perception of his role in normal life; the clever teacher does not choose to role-play the chief, leader, or judge, even though the children will expect this, since this is merely an extension of his role as teacher; instead he usually opts for messenger, guard or adviser, where he can control the action by subtle moves from below or behind. Theatre in education can free a wider range of reactions: the teacher is still the teacher, even when he is role-playing; the child's behaviour is still conditioned strongly by what he knows. For instance, in a dramatic situation involving provocation, children in an ordinary drama lesson invariably adopt one of two attitudes: some will shirk from provoking the 'character' because underneath they are afraid of the consequences of provoking the real person; the rest will over-react, enjoying the freedom from consequences that the drama brings. These are perfectly natural and justifiable responses, but in either case the drama gets lost, because the object of the conflict is the teacher himself, not the role he plays. This is not true of the actor/teacher; for the children his identification with his role is complete, and they can react safely and naturally within the drama. This applies just as much to presentation, where the reaction is projected, as to participation.

The whole subject matter of drama, by its very nature, can help the development of social perspectives. One of its main functions is to examine attitudes and create conscious awareness of relationships: of people to each other, to society and social institutions, morals and ethics, of how motivation leads to behaviour which leads to consequences. It highlights the pressure points and problem areas. This whole process will be dealt with in more detail in the next chapter, and is, in any case, implicit throughout TIE, so it should suffice now to give just one brief example. A programme which had enormous impact on its audience, called *You can't do That*, was about a young man torn between the long-term advantages of staying at school and college, and the short-term pleasures of leaving and earning money, between the wishes of his parents, of whom he was very fond, on the one hand, and on the other the esteem of his apparently independent elder brother and friends. It was hardly difficult for fifteen-year-olds to make the transfer and see what was relevant in it to themselves. It explored the hero's predicament in some depth, raising honestly the important conflicts, and holding them up impartially for examination, now this way, now that. Put down like this the subject-matter may seem dull and worthy, or trite and banal. In fact, it was a spectacularly theatrical programme, full of action and pace, with strong, economical characters and a framework of powerful, well-written songs in the audience's idiom.*[22]

An adult observer commented that the ending was predictable and melodramatic, but was instantly withered by the retort, 'Yes, well, you've probably seen too many plays, seen it all before. *We* didn't expect it, it was new to us and bloody good.' Total agreement from the class, total rout of the arrogant adult (me).

Chapter Four

TIE and specific educational practice

Problem-solving

'To learn how to think scientifically, i.e. solve problems, three major responses are required throughout the learning process:

1 Learning to recognise the situation as a problem and to withhold the emotional reaction of frustration.

2 Initiation of problem-solving behaviour immediately—a willingness to *try* to solve the problem.

3 Persistence in the development of problem-solving behaviour—to clarify the extent of the problem and possible solutions, and keep going until the problem is solved' (Jerome Bruner *et al.*).[23]

A particularly over-used phrase (over-used already in this book), beloved of modern educationists and teachers, is 'a problem-solving education'. In grandiosely claiming that educational drama, TIE, or any other discipline, can aid the development of problem-solving behaviour, it is easy to lull oneself into the belief that such activities as one provides are the only occasions when a child will meet and try to solve problems until he leaves school. Instead, surely, any need satisfied, desire achieved, or plan accomplished develops a new range of problem-solving activities. When a child wants a drink and drags a chair over to the tap, he is solving a problem. In a child's very early days, the emotional reaction of frustration is indistinguishable from the initiation of the problem-solving, as the parent responds to the first in order to satisfy the second: for example, quietens the baby by getting it a drink. Gradually the two become distinguished, when the parent is not around, or not co-operating, and from then on life is all problems, if you want to look at it that way. Even (perhaps especially) games court frustration voluntarily, where the possible satisfaction of success outweighs the disappointment of losing or failing. Reared on hide-and-seek, puzzle games and toys, as well as most parents' refusal to satisfy every immediate whim, most children come to school already conversant with playing the odds, besting opponents, beating systems and going through, round or over obstacles (except for the most extremely over- and under-indulged, for whose deprivation drama has a function more remedial and thera-peutic than the continuously educative).

Still, every little helps, and TIE can satisfy the second and third of the conditions quoted above by promising an exceptionally satisfying reward at the end. It says, 'problems can be fun', and explores the types of behaviour likely to solve problems in three different ways.

First, identification: in presented plays the audience goes through states of frustration as it identifies with the hero, and he or she is faced with a series of problems leading to some sort of resolution. Caught up in the action, if you were a child, you lived every moment of Beowulf's misfortunes. From the start you identified with him against his favoured blood-brother (you know what it is like to be ignored and despised; you would like to have his courage to challenge the slighters, and briefly, through the play, you can). With dignity he turned his back on his home to make his fortune (somehow, when you threatened in real life to run away the adults just laughed and offered you threepence). After a sea journey and shipwreck (you know the journey is exemplified by just streamers and material waving about while the actors rock, but nevertheless you are held breathless by their hypnotic colour and movement), he was welcomed to the stricken kingdom of Denmark where he offered to fight Grendel. (Here, the storyteller is acting as a comic, cowardly realistic foil, so that you can compare how you know you would really feel in these circumstances with Beowulf's indomitability, and you discover that grown-ups feel that way too.) Beowulf defeats Grendel (and when the monster appears you are 'really' just as frightened as the characters, it is so huge and horrible as it lurches towards you). Heroism succeeded heroism until (just as you are feeling that there is not much of a problem anyway, as Beowulf is bound to win so he is hardly worth supporting any more) suddenly he (and you too) was brought up sharply by humiliation and a warning against pride. The play moved to Beowulf's old age, and he was contrasted with a new character, Wiglaf, who was recognisably similar to the young Beowulf, so identification was now shared as Beowulf faced his last problem (and when beaten, as you know he is bound to be, unless the fantasy is silly, it does not matter, because the young Beowulf whom you loved and admired, the figure of yourself that you wish existed, still does exist, in Wiglaf). Wiglaf was left, holding aloft the emblem

The hero survives shipwreck (*Beowulf*)

of Beowulf, now his, and the Storyteller gently brought the children back, subdued, nervously worn out by the struggles they had undergone, the obstacles they had overcome.*[24]

Alternatively, the problem may be presented as performance, where identification or alienation may be involved, only to be left starkly unsolved, the solution lying in the minds of the audience: 'Did she leave, or didn't she?' The company may hope that the children will discuss it among themselves, or with the teacher:

'The clues are in what you have seen; now it is up to you to find out who murdered the King/what Duke William's real motives were/whether the defendant is guilty.'

The team themselves may set up the conditions for solving the problem—in discussion with the actors in or out of role, by a simulation exercise, or by specific follow-up work.

Finally, by participation, the children can be put in a problem-solving situation where they have to work together in order to solve a difficulty, like making the Wizard give back the keys (see page 4). An ingenious example of a programme which presented a series of problems to be solved, progressively more difficult and open-ended, was performed in three visits to a class of 44 eleven-year-olds, by a group of student-teachers.[25] During the programme the children met a space scientist and, avoiding the police for security reasons, helped find his assistant who had crashlanded during a mission. They became involved in a plot by enemy agents, were captured and escaped. Finally they met and assisted friendly aliens. On the first visit they were asked to solve a number of problems:

they had to read the map to discover where the capsule had landed;
they had to help (in mime) to mend a dismantled bus in which they were to travel to reach the landing-place;
they had to invent a cover story which would satisfy the police;
they had to uphold that story in the face of penetrating interrogation;
they had to approach the spacecraft with stealth, avoiding being discovered by the police, yet reaching it first;

they had to travel to a spare parts factory, help mend the machinery sabotaged by
enemy agents, and make the spare parts;
they had to end the visit with them all trapped inside the factory by enemy agents.

During the following week the children were invited to invent suitable strategies for
escape, a problem much more complicated than the others so far. Three emerged and
the second session was taken up with trying these out. The first two failed because of
flaws; the third succeeded and the mission was saved. On the third visit the children
met friendly aliens who challenged them to demonstrate what life on earth is like, a
problem where a great deal more initiative was required. The children built up in drama,
under the critical eyes of the aliens, an entire community, re-creating the life of the
factory, school, home, shops and so on.

This programme makes clear that there are considerable differences at least in degree
between the problems with which drama can face children. The simplest are the
'puzzles', with only one solution, like finding the doll, reading the map, fitting together
hidden messages or pictures. Similarly, it does not need much strategy to mend a bus,
put out a fire, or build a boat, though all of these co-operative activities need careful
organisation by the actors.

In some problems there is no one single solution; the children have a degree of choice
and invention, limited by the conditions of the drama. How can we escape from the
factory? What alibi will satisfy the police? How can we make the Wizard give up the
keys? The actors are the arbiters of acceptability, and if the plan is too 'easy', too glib,
then it will not succeed. Suppose the first plan is to drug the wizard with a con-
veniently invented invisible pill in his tea; then the Wizard decides not to drink his
tea today. In that case, the children dress up as ghosts to try to frighten him; but he
knows several ghosts, and these look far too solid, so it must be a trick by those noisy
children. In the third plan, two brave children dress up as a friendly witch from far-off,
with her cat; they call on the Wizard, on a clever pretext, and with difficulty lure
him away from the keys and his magic powder, then rush off, leaving him powerless,
to the great relief of everybody.

Solving problems like these always has a very simple satisfying outcome. Behind lies
the comforting 'philosophy of right answers', that everything eventually has a right
answer, or a rightful place, and if you try hard enough you will find it. This is fine

Chatting up the Wizard (*The Happy Land*)

Off to the manager's office (*A Hook, a Bob and a Four-letter Name*)

for infants, but when secondary programmes are still exhibiting this 'Bingo' mentality, they are not educating, they are lulling. Many primary programmes, in fact, start to take the problems they offer into a new dimension.

Decision-making

A documentary for ten-year-olds about the chequered history of London Docks[26] finished by showing their sad but inevitable decline. The children had been endowed over two visits as dock workers, with strong loyalties, and at the end they were faced with a choice of three courses of action:

either they could leave the docks, their life, with a redundancy benefit, and find work elsewhere;

or they could take a job at the new container terminal at Tilbury, uprooting themselves and their families from the traditionally close community of their friends;

or they could stay on for a while to help run down the dock, and when it eventually closed they would still get their redundancy pay, but all the best jobs might have gone.

As the ending of the play, each child had to go to the manager's office and sign on the list of his choice. There was no right answer; his decision depended on a thorough understanding of the implications of what he was doing, the advantages and disadvantages, modified by his own strength of feeling and loyalties. In performance, all three options were chosen, and interestingly, though the children did discuss their decisions among themselves, they very markedly did *not* automatically choose the same as their friends—a measure of their commitment to this unglamorous programme.

Here the decision was largely practical; junior children are quite capable of being faced with insoluble moral problems. In the programme *The Day of Fire*, where the children, as tribal villagers, had to decide whether to give two Strangers some precious water, the response of the Village Elders (the actor/teachers) depended not on the actual decision the village made, but on the depth and seriousness of the reasoning that led them to make it. If the Strangers reported as they came out that the children had just shown blank hostility, 'No, you can't have any and that's that', or casual agreement, 'The bowl's over there', responses implying a superficial involvement in the story, the Elders chided them strongly for either lack of hospitality or negligence. Usually, however, the argument was long and well-developed, and the Elders commended the children sympathetically.

Sometimes the children can be faced with a decision both moral and practical, and then they really are stretched intellectually. Later on in *The Day of Fire*, the children are left alone again with the Strangers, who are two scientists from Europe. The mysterious prescience of the Chief, a power he has just passed on to his chief-elect, one of the children, has saved them all from death in a volcano, and the scientists are privately determined to get this new chief back to Europe to find out the secret of this mysterious prescience of the Chief, a power he has just passed on to his Chief-elect, to accompany them back to Europe, ranging from blandishment, through bribery to blackmail. It is always a keen struggle, and more often than not the children eventually refuse. The theatrical ending that follows (one of two for either decision) conveys the warning that the Village is going to have to suffer the consequence of their decision.

Many times the company have asked the children afterwards if they would have preferred a happy resolution to the unsettling open end, but the children are always emphatic and unequivocal: 'It would not be right.' At one performance, a lady observer, used to happy endings in children's theatre overseas, and alarmed by the fierceness of this confrontation which clearly was not going to have one, stepped in bravely but inappropriately, role-playing a wild philosopher of the woods, with a solution full of harmony and universal brotherhood. The actor/teachers playing the scientists, who were still just in control of what they felt was very successful drama, were annoyed by the intrusion, and quickly phased the guru out, not too politely. Most of the children did not even notice her, and none of them reacted to her plan for happy resolution; her presence was, to them, irrelevant.

Moral understanding

As children grow older, it becomes less easy and less desirable to present problems of morality detached and abstracted from their contexts into fiction. Basic patterns of thought and reaction have been established, and exploration more often has to be in the realms of the familiar, offering new dimensions to what is 'known'. Most teenagers 'know' what they think of 'war', or 'old people', or 'gypsies'; their attitudes might not appeal to their teachers (or to gypsies, or old people) but those attitudes are valid for *them*. Looking into why they are valid, it is necessary to understand how attitudes are formed. Most attitudes are formed by individual experience; some are preconceptions (which can be just as strong), implanted by parents, friends, the media of communica-

Power passes to the Chief-elect (*The Day of Fire*)

tion like print and television, or teachers, in matters where the young person has no direct experience; some are the accepted attitudes of Society, or *his* society. By definition, attitudes are general rationalisations which, like any other generalisation, can be unhelpful or downright misleading in individual circumstances, and quite possibly more wrong than right, especially when they are based on one individual experience ('old people are a simple-minded little shrivelled woman called gran who gives us sweets when we have to go round on Sundays'), or on somebody else's preconception received third or fourth hand ('I don't like blacks; they come over here taking our jobs'—verbatim from the eleven-year-old son of a successful shopkeeper).

By offering a view of a subject calculated to challenge the preconceptions and pin down the attitudes, the TIE programme can do a useful service in opening doors. If it is didactic in tone or message it will probably fail, however, for older children and young adults quite rightly resent being told what to think, whatever the disguise; they suspect, often equally rightly, that you are trying to replace their preconceptions with your own, which may be just as faulty and unfounded on reality, merely from a different age or class perspective, which is why it is probably wisest for teams to steer clear of programmes on, for example, racialism, unless either they have a member who has personally experienced what being in a racial minority is like, or they do their homework very thoroughly with those who have experienced it.

Once aware of this danger, the team can arm themselves against speciousness or sentimentality, and bring programmes to challenge both stereotyped attitudes and indifference. Several recent programmes have quite successfully taken 'madness' as their theme: in one, *The Cullen Family*,[27] a girl is shown acting in a schizophrenic way, then a 'psychiatrist' takes us over her background in a simple series of flashbacks, which suggest reasons rather than apportion blame. The audience are then invited to talk to the characters. Though not always entirely successful in eliciting deep discussion, this simple programme certainly moved many of the audience to think beyond the attitude of 'madness is other people, nutters down at the funny farm'. (One spectator verbalised his impression as 'it's like a deep sulk'; a consultant surgeon observer, with long experience of mental illness, was very impressed by the accuracy of the programme, and endorsed the boy's words as showing real understanding of one kind of schizophrenia.) The whole range of contemporary stereotyped responses to madness are all grotesquely pilloried in another programme (Leeds Playhouse TIE's famous *Snap out of It*, by Roger Chapman and Brian Wilkes, published by Eyre Methuen, 1973), where the actors first assault the audience with the whole gamut of responses, at the terrific pace of frenzied non-stop revue; the audience laughs, but is not invited nor expected to make any moral comment. Then the members of the audience themselves are blind-folded and disoriented by being moved around the hall, around them disembodied voices quietly read aloud statistics of mental health, personal testimony, poems and articles on madness. No other comment is made, or needed. The response of one sixth-form student to one of the actors, which seemed to sum up the powerful atmosphere of subdued understanding at the end, was: 'I was going out to a party tonight, but I think I'm too miserable now. Thank you, I wouldn't have missed it for anything.' Two other secondary programmes chose formats similar to *The Cullen Family* to explore the subjects of suicide[28] and battered babies.[29] *The Ballad of Billy Martin* was one of two quite independent programmes in the same year and region on destitutes;[30] two other companies took the story of David Oluwale, an old black down-and-out driven to death by two policemen, for their subject-matter.[31]

This does not imply a lack or originality, or an excessive preoccupation with the grim and morbid—these were only a few of many varied programmes. It implies, rather, a willingness to use as material contemporary problems and preoccupations, and to present them in a way that can excite and stimulate the open minds of young people.

Emotional understanding

In a way, most of these programmes have a dual intention. Attitudes are not just states of mind, they are emotional reactions, strong conditioned reflexes linked to others, triggered off by mention of the subject to put up a rigid barrier which is also part of the image the individual presents to the world. By personalising a situation, and forcing (or asking) the members of the audience to shift their ground to look from the new angle necessary, the teams are seeking to turn these fixed conditioned reflexes into flexible emotional responses, constructive because they can receive a new experience on its own terms, creating the conditions for sympathetic understanding. All these programmes sought to show that 'madness', 'suicide', 'destitution' were not static and alien, but human, common, shifting and perhaps reversible states. Moreover, by choosing young and identifiable 'heroes', *The Cullen Family*, *The Ballad of Billy Martin* and the programme about suicide said: 'This could be you.' The last mentioned actually used a teenage girl co-opted from a nearby school to play its protagonist. *Snap out of It* asked the spectators to identify with the state of madness by thrusting them (those who wanted, anyway, there was no coercion) into a parallel state; blindness and madness both involve disorientation.

When companies go further and try to break down the strong generalised attitudes of society as a whole, destroying its taboos, they are on dangerous, though I would maintain vital, territory. The dangers often prove too daunting, as they did for the North Eastern team who started to prepare a programme on Mary Bell, the twelve-year-old Newcastle girl who murdered two infants in extraordinary circumstances.[32] The aim was to elicit the automatic and stereotyped reaction of fascinated horror which everybody's social training demands they produce to a story of this nature, and then sensitively and gently, but ruthlessly, peel it away and, by examining the case in depth, find some understanding of how and why it might have happened. The programme was designed round a song, whose last lines ran:

> 'So all you listening to my song, you know she knew the right from wrong,
> Her evil genius was strong, her punishment can't be too long,
> But also don't forget, please, that Mary could have been *you*.'

It was also intended to pose the question of what should be done with offenders like her (something the authorities have not yet answered to anybody's satisfaction). The instigator of this project, though aware that the subject would receive very mixed receptions from teachers and heads, had reckoned without the sensibilities of the team, including himself. Half the company wanted nothing to do with it from the outset; they found the whole concept of a play on that topic unacceptable either on principle, or because they did not want to handle such material themselves, or because they were worried about the local repercussions of material so close to home; instead, therefore, they set out to produce a puppet play for infants—very wisely, having such misgivings. The rest of the company started to work on the material, but several found it so explosive, so potentially obsessive, that it was first modified, then abandoned. This was entirely understandable, but perhaps a pity, because drama can, when handled responsibly, lend its own security to the exploration of 'unpleasant' or taboo subject-matter, and to be discomforting is sometimes the role of the secondary school educator, or it should be.

The emotional make-up of young people is not just a grey sludge of conditioned reflexes mixed with apathy. Each individual has areas which are very personal and filled with feelings he does not dare to exhibit, or even recognise, areas in particular of the negative emotions of anxiety, fear and guilt. A young urban boy of fourteen, caught up in the brash and aggressively masculine culture of his contemporaries, feels fright in spite of himself at his own potential power and independence, and his infantile longings for security; he has desperate trouble coming to terms with the demands of his new manhood, and sees no comfort in the confident faces around him (most of them determinedly showing no outward sign of identical anxieties—his own, to them, being equally bland). A play like the youth club programme *Simple Simon*[33] can be at least briefly reassuring as, in company with his friends and would-be friends, he watches a figure suffering as he suffers, bullied by the whole ethos of the Older, the Leader, the Powerful: pulled different ways by parental pressures, his sexual fantasies, the aloof reality of girls, his immediate desires, and his long-term ambitions to set the world afire. The 'victim' survives, and by surviving wins. With surprise and relief each member of the audience realises that the confident others around him have been identifying, too, with the victim, not his persecutor. This may be a reason, and comments from spectators suggest that it is, for this snappy programme's success in tough youth clubs.

Not every person watching one of the programmes about madness or suicide starts with unthinking attitudes or apathy. Within the audience there will be some who are already acquainted, or think they might be, with the despair of the suicide, or who, feeling the pull of obsessions and fragmentation of self, know 'that way madness lies'. A great deal of therapy for all kinds of psychological disorders and problems starts by trying to externalise, bring out into the open, the roots or at least the inner manifestation of the disorder. Once a dangerous unknown factor can be seen and recognised, it is no longer quite so dangerous; the patient can be on the way to accepting it as a natural part of his human condition rather than an irrepressible demonic force; then it often seems easier to make strategies to defeat or contain it. This idea has long been deeply rooted in drama, expressed perhaps inaccurately in theories of catharsis, that a play may, in a small way, momentarily, help people to come to terms with themselves.

Here again, the ice is thin, and clumsy treading over the fragile areas of other people's self-esteem can do more harm than good. When it is strangers putting their boots through and stirring up the depths it can be intrusive, impertinent and intensely embarrassing.

One team, who gave the impression that they were egotistically more concerned with ingratiating themselves than with any educative function, decided that everybody was interested in sex, and so an exploration of sexual fantasy would get the audience going. The result was merely prurient, and they did not even achieve their first intention, for the audience, after initially over-reacting in self-defence, relapsed into sullen boredom.†

A rather better programme for a different age group set out to tap the deep-rooted fears of infants, exploiting these gently and entertainingly, to give the children a little more security against their anxieties.[34] Ironically referred to as 'redundancy for infants' the programme started with the actors talking to the children, discussing being unwanted, or no longer needed (very close to the fears of children of this age). Quickly it was sublimated to story-telling, and characters emerged. Eventually the children were shown a funny and exciting presentation about three forgotten and redundant people: a chimney sweep, a pedlar and a princess. If anything, trying to avoid the heavy boots of the programme previously described, this one trod too lightly, making it rather effortless to watch.

Subject disciplines

'All those sub-psychological aims are very well, but hardly relevant in the schoolroom, possibly very inappropriate there', that dedicated and overworked French teacher might well be saying at this point. 'Children still need knowledge and skills far more specific than have been mentioned yet; the real world is cold for those who cannot wrap up warm in examination certificates, even if they are sane, balanced individuals full of sympathy for everything (and anyway, it has already been emphasised that the socialising effect of all this drama is infinitesimal). Why, then, should I supervise somebody else's class while mine, who need every grammatical minute I can give them, are down in the hall being straightened out by a crowd of strangers, most of whom look rather young. What is there in it for me?'

Bearing in mind the frequency of TIE visits to any one school at the moment, one must reply, 'Very little at present, but do not despair.' Giving help with the learning process of specific subject disciplines is a very important part of the work of TIE teams. Your sixth form might be one of the fortunate ones to be visited by an interesting-sounding venture called *Frogs begin at Calais*.[35] This consists of short extracts from plays by Racine, Marivaux and Anouilh, part of the 'Chanson de Roland', and poems by Rimbaud, put together quite logically, and linked by a witty and oblique theatrical look at French history and obsessions. The passages were chosen equally as highlights from probable examination texts and as illustrations of the obsessions. Languages teachers wrestle nobly with tape recorders and projectors, struggle to fit in inconvenient radio and television programmes, or play the annual game of chance called 'Pick the Assistant Français', all in an effort to give their children the opportunity of direct contact with foreign languages. Unlike the rare and very localised visits of theatre groups like the Comédie Française, a TIE programme can be tailored to the exact needs of the children watching it, even if they are starting from scratch. Looking for an interesting way to approach the teaching of Welsh for eight-year-olds who had no knowledge of it at all, the Welsh Language adviser of one education authority asked his local TIE team for help. They were given the very specific task of introducing thirty common words, used in a grammatical context, and repeated often enough to become familiar. This put a number of severe restrictions on the group; for one thing, there was no getting away from the amount of sheer teaching that would be needed, with the resultant threat to the theatricality of the experience. This was solved by giving the play a circus background, where the children were invited to play various games (all involving the use of language) with a couple of endearing clowns; the only natural Welsh speaker in the team was cleverly cast as the Ringmaster, a role where authority and control, as well as the demand for high standards all the time, would be entirely in character. The circus was threatened by a dragon who ate Welsh words (and occasionally children); with the help of an English-speaking inventor, who had himself to be assisted to learn Welsh, the dragon was defeated, and the circus games restored. Put baldly, this plot is thin and artificial; in practice it was entirely successful. The storyline provided the initial impetus, the clowns, Pog and Mog, kept the children captivated, the dragon filled them with pleasurable fear, and by the end the words and sentence structures had been drummed in quite painlessly but very thoroughly; the simplicity was not banal, but perfectly economical.[36]

In a totally different area of the curriculum, a programme within the strictest definition of learning skills, touring a few months before decimal currency was introduced, took classes of top infants, one at a time, and familiarised them with the new money. Naturally

Pog, Mog and the Inventor (*Syrca Sulwen*)

they participated in *New Pence for Old*,[37] shopping and paying for what they had bought at the market, just as they would practise in class, but much more memorably.

Perhaps unexpectedly, Physical Science is well served, with at least two companies in recent years catering entirely for its interests. At one end, The Molecule Club, an offshoot of London's Mermaid Theatre, gives performances which are somewhere between an animated science lesson and a theatrical show. The other company, founded by a university Professor of Mathematics, explores the further reaches of relativity and religion through the medium of plausible science fiction plays.[38]

Music in the infants' school, puppet-making and road safety are all topics of simple teaching that have been attempted with some success in TIE. Still at the level of purveying facts, programmes often are capable, alongside their main purpose, of clarifying muzzily-understood concepts, feeding in more information on subjects such as how local government works, what exactly it is that social workers do, or the ramifications of house purchase and renting.

History

One of the curricular subjects that TIE has fastened on as a perfect outlet for its skills right from the beginning is History, and over the years programmes either with a primarily historical content and context or invoking historical background have threatened to outnumber all other programme subjects put together. To children for whom history means a grim chronological plod, starting with the Romans and just about getting up to the nineteenth century for O-level, which was the History teacher's special study at college so he knows enough of that to get them through on his notes, a TIE programme can be an oasis of delight, and will teach more in an hour than the twenty pages of copied text-book, the traced drawing of a contemporary gun, house, or costume, and the work-sheet, supposed to make the subject more interesting, that just entail a trail along to the library for a different text-book from which to copy. This ghastly parody of course does gross injustice to the many thrilling projects and imaginative teachers to be found, especially in primary school classrooms. It is, however, quite accurate for two schools of my knowledge, and in some measure for many, many more.

On the simplest level, the theatrical presentation can literally make history come to life; a linear concept, such as that shown overleaf,

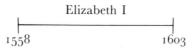

Elizabeth I

1558   1603

can be shown to be a woman of three dimensions, with a tough, shrewd mind, uncertain temper and teeth that hurt, having to cope with a man she had loved who had gone off and raised a rebellion. In one famous programme, *The Bolton Massacre*,[39] the children were sitting quietly in their classroom when the door was flung open, and two men, imposingly dressed as recruiting sergeants, one a Cavalier, the other a Roundhead, strode in. They divided the class up between themselves and each took his group off to opposite ends of the school, where for half an hour he taught the children musket and sabre drill, working them very hard physically, feeding in one-sided facts and opinions, and establishing a fierce partisan loyalty. From this hectic beginning, the pace hardly slackened: seventeenth-century Bolton was conjured up and peopled, regular army life explored, the children taught traditional weaving skills with a working replica. Of course there was a battle, cleverly structured to allow each child some freedom of action while still achieving historically the right result. Finally, the villain of the massacre was captured and arraigned in front of the people of Bolton, who tried him and gave their verdict. Though history gives one verdict, the children were allowed to make up their own minds as, now with profound understanding, they debated the issues of military and political expediency, how far a leader is responsible for atrocities committed in wartime, and to whom he is responsible. Only afterwards was the historical decision revealed, as an interesting sidelight on the similarity or difference between how people thought then and now.

The last part of this programme adds another dimension to the basic historical reconstruction. First showing us 'what it was like then', it goes two steps further, saying 'why it was like this' and asking 'what has this to say to us now?' This, surely, is one of the most important purposes of teaching history. I must admit that, as a mere adult on whom the programme had been demonstrated, when a while later news broke of the My Lai massacre in Vietnam I found myself thinking of *The Bolton Massacre*; I am sure it clarified my outlook.

As well as concentrating on narrow areas of history, particularly battles and incidents,

The townsfolk defend themselves (*The Bolton Massacre*)

TIE can present very entertainingly a whole panorama, to give a rounded perspective: every Dublin schoolboy knows about the Great Famine and the Easter Rising, more hazily about Parnell and Pearse, very vaguely about the Act of Union and The Pale. Gathering these strands of Irish history together, cutting out the mass of related facts and fantasies, and arranging them in a sequence which emphasised the continuity and inevitability of the process, a typical 'model' emerged as the framework of a programme.[40]

Holding up the present for scrutiny through the eyes of the past was the aim of a programme written to honour the thirteen-hundredth anniversary of the birth of the Venerable Bede, and performed on Tyneside and Wearside, often in schools bearing his name, which are frequent round there.[41] The programme took his contribution to bringing scholarship within the reach of many ordinary people, and compared ironically his high hopes with the golden age now that everybody can read and write. The moral seemed to be that history teaches very little.

A historical perspective may have a secondary value as necessary background to an understanding of an aspect of contemporary life, so a programme about the role of trade unions today started with a theatrical montage of how they developed, from the mediaeval guilds (questionably their ancestors), via Peterloo and the Match Strike, up to the Industrial Relations Act of 1971. Locally-based teams are in a particularly good position to help the children to understand their own heritage and environment; directly or indirectly, the car industry is vitally important to children living in Coventry, many of whose fathers and mothers actually depend on it for their livelihoods (and the Docks for people living in East London, and mechanisation and the drift away from the country for rural children). Programmes on all these subjects had a high historical content, used to highlight the situation and problems of today. *Made in Coventry*[42] and *A Hook, a Bob and a Four-letter Name*[26] (about London Docks) both used the same technique of endowing the children as workers in the industry, experiencing the vicissitudes of expansion and slump, using occupational mime, from the eighteen-nineties gradually moving forward in time until the present day.

The emphasis, then, is not necessarily 'History' as a discipline in itself. It can figure as a primary element, as a factor for comparison, or merely as a background. It can even act just as a jumping off point, as it does in the programme *Play With Fire*,*[43] about the nineteenth-century 'Mad Martin' brothers, one of whom tried to burn down York Minster; another was an eccentrically brilliant inventor, and the third an even

Lock-out at the car factory (*The Carmakers*)

more erratic and talented painter. History provided the plot; Victorian religious revivalism and the conditions in mental asylums made the background to what developed into a study of madness, letting the careers of these three brothers ask the audience to consider: 'Who was the sanest? Is anybody sane? What is sanity?'

History well deserves and must maintain its traditionally sacrosanct position of high status on the timetable when it can serve the following functions (all of which TIE can help to service):

transmitting to children some awareness of how their world has become as it is; showing them examples of the consequences of human behaviour, behaviour they can understand because it is the motives and actions of people a little like themselves; helping them to an interested realisation of the importance of factors which, unseen, dominate their lives: political and economic pressures, social and personal drives; providing them with touchstones to compare and evaluate the present, and to develop a consistent sense of proportion.

Cultural heritage

A child's heritage certainly consists partly of these historical and social forces, but history is not his only legacy. Abstract perspectives derived from fact and the interpretation of facts are a fairly sophisticated intellectual pursuit. Much earlier and perhaps more important touchstones come through the stories, legends and mythology which provide through their symbols the fusion of emotional and cerebral responses into a stable, ordered acceptance. This has already been stated as a major function of children's stories, but there is another dimension: each society has its particular mythological code of reference, which unconsciously affects thought and communication. This common stock of reference allows an extra medium of communication, a shorthand of symbols on which much of the language depends: 'herculean', 'the patience of Job', 'elves and pixies'. The archetypes of the Blackfoot Indians and the Ancient Hebrews may be the same deep down, and for that reason it is valuable for a child to read or experience the creation legend of the Blackfoot. It is more important still for him to experience the stories of the Bible, of Classical mythology and Celtic legend, if he is an Anglo-Saxon child, because these form one of the basic layers of his own culture, which he shares with all those around him, his family and his historical background.

Hindu and Christian children can sit together enjoying a play about Sita and Vishnu and a play about the life of Jesus, but not equally; each play will mean more to one than to the other, each set of mythological symbols carries underlying it a set of attitudes.

Literature and the arts

An understanding of the *common* attitudes of a culture becomes particularly important when children grow older and approach all the arts, social studies and history itself, critically. In particular, theatre in education can help with the appreciation of literature, especially drama. Theatre groups of all kinds, when presenting a 'standard' or famous play, often preface it with some kind of workshop, or finish with a discussion, feeling that if they do not, much of importance will be lost on an audience which lacks many of the necessary reference points. 'Hard' writers from Shakespeare to Beckett are nearly always given this treatment. A local English theatre was presenting Sean O'Casey's *Juno and the Paycock*, set in Ireland during the Troubles, as a major company programme in the adult theatre; it happened also to be a set book for many of the schoolchildren in the area (a fact of box-office relevance not ignored). The TIE team attached to the theatre presented a 'back-up' programme on Irish history, a subject of which they might assume many of the students would be entirely ignorant.[44] The purpose and therefore the whole emphasis of this programme was quite different from the Dublin programme on the same subject: there it was to clarify and give perspective to the students' own historical heritage, to which they would already have a shared emotional attitude; here it was mainly to give sufficient background knowledge of a largely unknown and alien culture for students to appreciate the play. In other cases, it has been thought useful to give a theatrical biography, entertaining and critical, of an author such as Dylan Thomas or Charles Dickens; great composers have had the same treatment, camped-up from a group for whom show was rather more important than content.

An extension of this is to take a work of literature itself and present it so that it is directly aimed at a particular audience, which usually means updating it. This is popular with works that might seem intractable for twentieth-century youth, like 'The Rape of the Lock', with its classical imagery and Augustan attitudes (one cannot expect infant TIE and storytimes to have familiarised all one's sixth formers with enough classical mythology for that!), or *The Pilgrim's Progress*. The danger, of course, is that one does not explain the author's attitudes, merely removes them, leaving an empty shell, or may perhaps replace them with vapid twentieth-century attitudes (one's own, or what one imagines to be the students'), vapid because they are inevitably ill-fitting and artificially imposed.

Language

If TIE can help, minutely, in perpetuating the common stock of symbolic reference, that already gives it a function in language development. It can go further than this, creating through participation conditions where the actors and the drama set up opportunities for sustained language flow that really stretches the children's powers of language. In programmes like *The Bolton Massacre* and *She's Leaving Home* the discussion is intense and long-drawn-out, but never long-winded; in *The Day of Fire* the final confrontation once took over half an hour with no slackening of intensity and little repetition, and no falling-out of bored children; groups continually broke off and argued among themselves, joining up later; children, normally quiet and withdrawn, discovered powers of persuasion and rhetoric that amazed their teachers and even themselves under the emotional influence of their identification. This drawing out of shy or disaffected children is a common feature of TIE, a virtue cunningly exploited in a programme designed by a college team for one class of uninterested fourteen-year-old girls, who showed at best no interest and at worst antagonism to their school life, including drama.[45] The actor/teachers presented a succession of short plays, each with easily recognisable, identifiable characters and an obviously strong dramatic shape (beginning, middle, climax, end), except the last. This playlet was about a woman who brought home a baby not her own; her husband treated her with kindness, and conversation with her doctor revealed that she was undergoing acute depression after the death of her own child, and was convinced that this baby was hers. At this point the actors disingenuously stepped out of role and 'admitted' that they could not think up any worthwhile ending to the play. They invited the girls, who were by now caught up in the dramatic convention as well as the very emotive and well-aimed subject matter, to help them to work out an ending. They split the class into small discussion groups. The girls apparently rose quite willingly to the bait, discussed the issue earnestly and uninhibitedly explained and debated their solutions in public. (With even more cunning subterfuge, the team eventually had them physically participating in a way described later.)

TIE gives young children an opportunity more exciting than class storytime (which is appreciated, but in a different way, as a regular pleasant routine) both to listen to and then practise language as a powerful tool. In *I Say*,[46] a programme for immigrant children later adapted for use with young infant classes, the actor/teachers told the children stories in several different ways, using puppets, sound effects, occupational mime and narration, pictures, even total mime as a contrast. Then they asked the children, for follow-up work, to try making up stories of their own in various ways. Some days later the team returned and talked to the children about their work; the language flow was very impressive as the children delightedly described their creations to the sympathetic team. Finally the team presented a last story as a piece of straight theatre.

Language development does not stop in the junior school, and the theme of *The Global Village Daily News*[47] for articulate senior secondary school students was the dangerous power of language to persuade and pervert as well as to communicate. Techniques of bias and half-truth, insincere emotion and selective language were explored within the framework of a newspaper that the audience helped to write.

The language training can be very specific: 'men' applying for a job are interviewed by characters (actor/teachers) who put them through searching tests that give the pupils a taste of interview procedure. A group of 'workers' putting in a pay demand need to explain clearly to the management what they want and why they want it; the 'management' have to be equally careful drafting their reply; a basic understanding of the processes and perils of negotiation emerges.

The actor/teachers have to be always alert themselves, using language that heightens the situation, and giving the children an example to listen to and follow. Though in presentation this is as far as the immediate language responsibility goes, whether presentation or participation, infant or sixth form, the language development function is essentially the same in all cases: to give the children a conscious understanding of the importance, flexibility and power of the spoken word. Dramatic conflict provides both the need for language and the motivation, theatricality provides the setting to hear it used at its most powerful, while participation provides the tools, the context and the confidence to practise it.

Imaginative development

In a way this heading speaks for itself, because whenever ideas are being broadened, new horizons made to appear, and children's powers to express these new perceptions increased, the conditions for imaginative development defined in the last chapter are being fulfilled. Teams have occasionally set up situations much less structured than usual, in order to give the children a chance to work more freely, in a way much closer to an educational drama lesson. Several companies have hit on the idea of using cardboard cartons or similar debris as a starting point; in one case, the actors as 'Inventors' ask the children to invent anything they like with their boxes; another character arrives and introduces the thinnest of storylines, just enough to direct the children's work so that it progresses, without noticeably affecting their freedom—to them it is merely another interesting idea to include in their playing.[48]

This element of structure, however loose, in imaginative play, is very important for keeping the dynamic elements of drama and theatricality (which can only exist where there is progress) and for maintaining the heightened learning situation: on the one hand, you cannot look at a tableau for ever, and on the other, if you are going to offer total freedom of play and experiment, you might as well send the children out into the playground, pack up and go home. Educational drama derives its justification from the theory that the elements which the adults can offer add direction and control to the children's ideas, guiding them further and deeper into new levels of perception; that is the learning process. Theatre in education offers an extra element: the adults' ideas as the basis for the game itself. This is why a totally unstructured context does not always work, as some well-intentioned teams have discovered when they bring a situation, a character, or even a box of hats into a classroom or playground, with nothing so decadent as a preconceived idea, and leave it entirely up to the children to make the running. Occasionally it might work; the man with a limp in a funny hat, or the group standing round looking down at a dead (stuffed) dog might provide enough spark for particularly inventive children. Often, though, the actor ends up by hastily structuring the situation, to protect himself from either over-excited anarchy or creeping loss of interest. A sense of the importance of having a sub-structure is clear in the comments of the team on *The Inventors*:

'The child progresses from working on *his* invention where any answer is right to *our* invention where he has to use his skill in a social context. Once they became confident in working with boxes the children began automatically to build a story and include characters round their own inventions.'

Other teams have used items like a sword, an envelope with a mysterious message, and an enormous net as their jumping-off point into structured imaginative play. Still others have used a character, such as a scruffy old woman sitting motionless in the middle of the hall; if the children do approach her, she will provide the sketchiest of contexts, a problem which the children may solve in any way they wish; they may prefer to respond in another way, say by hostility or contempt, in which case they still have a problem—she is still there in the middle of the hall inhibiting their game.

Remedial and corrective

Up to a point this loose kind of inventive play is very appropriate for children in schools for the especially deprived, disabled, or maladjusted. Being close to children's play, it can help them to learn to play constructively, in which ability, whether by cause or effect, they are often deficient. Because in many cases the capacity for sustaining play of these children is so limited, it might however be wiser at first to have a fairly definite structure. The last programme described above[49] was designed for infants in an educationally subnormal school; the theatrical element of the old woman was really meant to lead into an educational drama situation, but it rather petered out in practice, after a very powerful opening ten minutes, because it lacked the continuing theatricality to maintain the special interest it had aroused, and the children could not provide this. Had it been an ordinary educational drama lesson throughout, the conditions might have been different; the context would have been the children's from the beginning, with their regular teacher in his regular over-all role, and no expectations of a theatrical event would have been raised. As it was, it took them into the actors' territory and rather left them there.

Children with special needs or deficiencies are often capable of identifying much more strongly than normal children; rationalising, questioning and disbelief are less well-developed. The hatred generated towards the villainous Mr Grim[50] in one E.S.N. school was so intense that when he was routed the actors had difficulty getting him off unharmed; afterwards, by chance, several large lads saw him through a classroom window, alone, changing out of his costume, and turned ugly; though he had locked the door they picked up sticks and rocks and were undecided whether to lie in wait for him, or break through the window, when a teacher came to the rescue. As he drove away (along with the heroine they were so loyal to, and all the other actors), they menaced his car.

TIE, as well as language and ideas practice, may be able to give brief help in the development of motor skills; children with poor spatial ability, some of them very defensively lazy in class, loved finding the pieces of the king's broken picture and spent a very long time absorbed in fitting it together.[51] In one performance of *The Happy Land* at a spastics' centre, the high point of the programme was finding and building the doll; those who could walk swarmed everywhere, the princess had to leap for safety as wheelchairs hurtled busily past, while some children who could neither walk nor talk properly nonetheless found ways of keeping the nurses holding them busy scurrying round.

The surface of this whole important educational area, like that of teaching subject skills through TIE, has barely been scratched, however. One or two specialist companies do exist, such as the National Theatre for the Deaf (whose primary aim is anyway rather different); links are forged here and there with local authority special education advisers, Health and Social Services Departments, so that established local companies do try to squash an occasional programme for special education into their crowded schedules. It can nevertheless be said with some justification that in pursuing the wider aims of education, TIE is perhaps rather neglecting the narrower and more readily obtainable objectives.

Social values and criticism

In the secondary school especially there is no shortage of programmes on the grandest or most nebulous of topics. Examining contemporary social values is, one way or another, the staple diet of the secondary programme, whether tragical, comical, historical, pastoral, and so on. The educational purposes of all these programmes seem to fall into one of three categories, which invariably correspond to the companies' political (or Political) outlook.

At one extreme, once popular and now rather discredited, is the kind of programme which by examining certain social values helps the audience to come to terms with them and accept them. In these, the Hero, child of Samuel Smiles out of Mother Nature, and usually second cousin to Candide (but without Voltaire's irony) experiences the Cruel Indignities and Harsh Injustices of the World, struggles with his Baser Self, evolves his Better Nature, and emerges a New Man. This kind of programme never has any difficulty being accepted by the most dyed-in-the-wool head-teachers; it is proving less acceptable nowadays to its audiences.

At the opposite pole, the Hero as Victim (by Brecht out of Mother Necessity) is more popular with teams, less so with teachers; the Hero is not the eventual master of his Destiny, but is crushed by the Cruel Indignities, Harsh Injustices and so on. Never mind; Things Would Be Different If . . . and the Red cavalry is seen on the horizon.

Most companies, pedlars of praxis, eschew both these doctrinaire positions and neatly choose an ambivalent position: an aspect of society, such as woman's role in present day life, some perspective on poverty, pollution, or one of those social attitudes already mentioned (madness, the generation gap, and so forth) is examined critically, often satirically. The subject is 'opened up', and the audience challenged to question accepted values, but not necessarily to reject them. The dilemma is usually made as difficult as possible, and even if the company is strongly committed to one side, to reform or revolution, at least one door is always left open, the audience invited to reject the programme's message. This kind of programme is invariably less simply satisfying than the other two, and frequently leaves students asking in vain for answers, irritated by being left in the air.

There, in practice, are the alternatives: you can give right answers, you can give other right answers or you can give no answers at all; you take your pick of which you think is most educative according to your predilection. It is worth bearing in mind that, if you have a message, though the techniques of theatre are powerful selling aids, no theatrical expertise in the world can stop an audience rejecting it if it is ultimately unacceptable. To refer back to where we started, the company sees the members of the audience for an hour or two; but their outlooks on life are the result of over a decade of living.

'Young people's theatre is concerned with the *child of today* and the kind of adult he will develop into. It is concerned with extending and enriching a child's enjoyment and experience of life, and with developing his sensibilities to prevent him being swamped by today's mass influences' (Roger Chapman).[52]

This statement, made by one of the leading exponents of theatre in education, is true, the last part as far as it goes, and it gives a clue to the highest (unfortunately the woolliest, too) aim that TIE, as I see it, can aspire to. It can start young people coming to terms with the unresolvable philosophical problems which trouble everybody, consciously or not. It can bring out for open examination the conflicts between an individual's freedom of choice and his social responsibilities, with the many levels and kinds of freedom and responsibility inherent in that. It can help make individuals aware of the strong closing pressures exerted on them, the manipulative influences. Roger Chapman was right to mention 'today's mass influences', but contemporary ad-mass is not the only force that threatens individual autonomy; since time began, man has been subject to the power of custom and tradition, the forces which uphold society and stifle change. By showing the possibilities, and the dangers, of change, and holding up alternatives for comparison, theatre in education can momentarily offer to individuals who make up an audience the choice between the discrimination that brings risk and the conformity that offers security.

Chapter Five

The perils and pleasures of participation

'Participation has come to suggest scenes of yelling and over-excitement—actors and teachers know that it is the easiest thing to bring out a child's violence; it is quite another matter to offer him moments of heightened experience and to ensure that such moments do not evaporate before the child has had a chance to explore fully their significance to himself' (J. Dudley).[53]

No single aspect of the development of TIE has caused such a storm of controversy and polarisation as the use of audience participation. The very phrase has almost everybody leaping to defend one or other flag, ready to fire off a volley of lethal generalisations at the enemy. Many of those people concerned with upholding the quality of the theatrical experience feel that this is incompatible with 'education by doing', that each weakens the other, that the essences of theatre are identification and concentration, and any intrusion of the audience's selves into the drama distracts their ability to project their feelings on to the characters. In certain circumstances these people may be right, but it is not so simple. Participation can certainly change the nature of the theatrical experience in a number of ways. It does not always do so; when young children, at a gripping moment in a show, leap up and shout out to warn their hero of the danger looming behind him, it is merely a spontaneous overflow of their powerful identification being expressed. Many shows deliberately play for these moments, and the children, recognising them, respond dutifully and enthusiastically, 'Look out, behind you!', or 'Oh no, it isn't!' This has become ritualised into part of the convention (often implying rather superficial involvement, too). So far, no change. Does change automatically signify weakening? Many disillusioned drama advisers and emotionally bruised actors will testify that badly-handled participation may indeed weaken the theatrical impact in one of two ways: either by whipping up a superficial excitement, and encouraging the children into a display of released tensions during which the play drowns, or by intruding the participation elements into the play, during which the tension seeps away and the identification is lost.

However, it may sometimes change the conditions of the theatrical experience to enhance it, add a supplementary dimension, or alter the children's perception of it, so that although the theatricality may be proportionally less, it is just as powerful in itself. At the least, it can add an extra dimension which can exist alongside the theatricality, perhaps not enhancing it, but not harming it either. At its best, I maintain that the improvisation and the theatricality feed each other, growing together into a fusion of personal experience and projected identification, completely subjective but with its own sense of proportion, more complete and more thoroughly affecting than any presentation.

Having fired which rash salvo, I am bound to admit that such moments are few over-all (though commonplace to the best companies) and much of what is temptingly billed as 'active participation' is just as 'superficial and limited ... tatty and sloppy ... insipid and meaningless ... a sad compromise' as some disappointed and exasperated drama advisers say it is.

It seems to me that there are three main types of 'participation', each of which has a relationship to the central theatrical experience entirely different from the others; within these types are numerous differences in the degree and percentage of participation used, even differences in kind defined by different objectives. And this is before one starts making value judgments. There are one or two problematic areas where the categories overlap, but not many. It is, of course, possible to use more than one degree or even type of participation within one programme. I would define the over-all categories as:

Extrinsic, where the element of participation is separated from the theatricality.

Peripheral, where the audience is invited to contribute in order to add to the theatricality without affecting either the structure and nature of the play or its own basic function as audience.

Integral, where the audience perspective becomes also the perspective of characters within the drama, especially when the audience members act as well as being acted upon. The structure of the dramatic conflict, the audience's relative position to it, and therefore the total experience are altered. The element of theatre is no longer central.

Extrinsic participation

The simplest and most traditional way to involve the audience actively is to hold a discussion after the performance. This has the obvious advantage of being a two-way process, giving actors feedback from the members of the audience, discovering how much they have enjoyed or understood the play, which sections have been most successful; this is particularly useful in a home-made and flexible programme which can be changed accordingly. Discussion seems to have other factors in its favour. It is a treat for the young people to talk to real actors, which should provide an initial interest; if the programme has been provocative, children or students will have an opportunity to test out their own points of view against each other and the cast; the company can correct any serious misconceptions and explain confusions. Almost automatically, then, schools' matinees and particularly secondary schools' programmes 'will be followed by a general discussion'.

As a rule, in my experience, discussion is the most over-rated and unsatisfactory form of participation. It rarely fulfils any of these intentions, and it is often actively harmful. It might be said that a post-mortem is not really part of the live play, so it does not matter. This is erroneous; as far as the audience is concerned, it is another part of the totality which starts when they take their seats and finishes when they file out. The reasons for failure are several, and not hard to find, but the main one is that if the programme has been successful, with a satisfying climax of one sort or another, then almost by definition anything that follows is an anti-climax. A play will raise issues and explore them in the heightened atmosphere of the drama, and the issues will register on the audience emotionally as well as intellectually. The audience is not necessarily going to want to verbalise coolly about something which, if the playwright and company have done their job, is powerful and complete in itself; what remains is picking over the carcase. If, on the other hand, the programme has not been successful and the audience is confused or irritated, then the spectators are not going to be bothered to go over it another way and be shown how wrong they are; they know that it has not worked on its own terms. The same applies to confusing sections of an otherwise satisfying programme: a few, certainly, may be curious and appreciate explanation; many others prefer to put it down to experience and just remember the credits, knowing that, even if the part which confused them is discussed, there is no guarantee that an explanation in words will be worth the effort, or any less confusing.

The charisma of an actor's presence can be over-rated, too, and this can work against the success of after-show discussions: to begin with, the glamour of the actor is nothing compared with the glamour of the character he played, so, when he steps out of role—again, anticlimax. The skills needed to appear prepossessing in open interaction are not necessarily the same as an actor's, and disillusion can quickly set in. Besides, plays are as long as they need to be; when they are over, the audience has usually had enough, so the actors need to give a spell-binding performance—in their own personae, without the help of role—to stop the children thinking of their sore bottoms, wondering if it is dinnertime, or just wanting to stretch their legs and run around.

It *is* possible to have successful discussions, and even to plan for them to avoid the pitfalls above. The most obviously effective way is deliberately to structure the programme so that the discussion is an integral part: the climax, or at least the natural outcome. This is particularly feasible with open-ended senior work, where the issues can be presented in a challenging way that will leave the students longing for an opportunity to express their opinions. Even when this has been achieved, the problems are not all solved. Encouraging constructive discussion is a subtle and delicate art, as any experienced teachers sensitive to group and personal needs know, but too many actors and teachers patently do not. There are two main dangers, but both spring from a basically self-centred approach to the concept of the discussion, and both are rationalisations of the actors' fears and desire for security: in other words, self-defence reflexes.

It is important for the actors to be aware of the degree of their own emotional commitment to the programme, and to beware evangelism. The programme should have communicated its own message, definite or equivocal, and it will have its own clearly-defined responses from the individuals in the audience, who will want to express these responses in their own way. It is unconsciously very tempting to lead off with a homily, recapitulating the story and painstakingly emphasising the moral or the argument. Ostensibly to get the discussion going, it is the shortest cut to absolute silence; the audience is left feeling either 'That's it, then', or 'Since they so obviously want us to think this way, there's not much point in arguing with them.'

Suppose the actors steer clear of that pothole, another is ahead. A proportion of the students is bound to have a negative response of one kind or another: some will violently disagree with the moral, or with the way the conflict has been presented; others will be confused about or misunderstand even the best programme; other still will have some tangential response whose relevance will be very difficult to see, especially on the spur of the moment, but is nevertheless real to the individual. Faced with these responses, it takes an actor or a teacher almost superhuman willpower not to react in one of two ways equally absurd in retrospect. Leaping to the defence of the material which one has spent a long time writing and rehearsing, either one slaps down the response by tedious exposition and reiteration, 'No, you have not got the point, listen . . .', or one goes further and overstates the case. Receiving an intelligently sceptical reaction from sixth formers to a programme which was already a glib and tendentious attack on the techniques of advertising,† one team found themselves driven in its defence to suggest that all forms of publicity were dishonest and evil, all consumers gullible idiots. It is worth at all times remembering that the response of children and young people, lacking the sophisticated tolerance of their elders, is usually an honest one, and not necessarily as negative as it sounds (even unbiased adult interviewers use the trick of attacking an idea to probe it in depth). In fact, the only dishonest response children tend to make is too easy acceptance of the programme's ideas (seeking adult esteem by agreeing with adults' ideas) and *this* is the response which should be recognised and jolted. If, on the other hand, the aggressive negativism of the questions shows the students not disposed to take the discussion seriously, it had better be hurriedly abandoned.

The actors need to be very sensitive to the motives behind all questions; they should always start disposed to be sympathetic and supportive, but not afraid to seek amplification if necessary. Any child who speaks up in front of a whole audience is risking a lot, and may not be very good at expressing himself first time. Comments should generally be accepted as sincere and any validity emphasised; questions should be answered as briefly and as clearly as possible, because it is easy to drown a child with words. It may be necessary to repress an attention-seeker, or somebody deluded but stubborn, who is holding up the discussion unwarrantably; this is a delicate defusing operation, to subdue without humiliating, because resentment quickly spreads. Children wanting to speak, but not having quite the courage or drive to get in before the fluent and disputatious, need to be spotted and room made for their contributions. Above all, nobody should be coerced: 'How about you, yes, you over there, what do *you* think?'

Everybody has a reason for not speaking and should be allowed the right to remain silent. If, after the leaders have made reasonable efforts, *nobody* wants to speak, this should be accepted quietly and naturally, without implanting any sense of failure—for all one knows, the programme *was* enough, and the rest is going on in the minds of the audience. So often one sees unhappy actors and perspiring teachers flogging a dead horse, going to extremes of cruelty to make it trot. I recall a performance of a pro-gramme about women in society,† really written for sixth forms, to about fifty fourth-year boys and girls. It was witty but sophisticated, and very long. At the end the audience had had enough, many of them long before the end. After a break, which in any case took their minds off the subject, they had to return for a 'discussion'. Valiantly, but vainly and rather ineptly, the actors tried to spark off discussion about women's roles, but the students would not talk: as well as the team and their teachers, several visiting strangers were present; any impressions which the students had received were rather nebulous and mixed up, so they had no intentions of putting their heads on the block of possible ridicule, especially from the other sex and from these strangers. The teacher then took up the struggle with a jaunty confidence which was clearly forced and which the students equally clearly resented. As their housemaster, he felt safe in the field of personal relationships, so he cheerily asked the students whether their mothers worked, whether they wanted children when they were married, whether they preferred free love to marriage, 'Hands up all those who believe in free love', how many were contemplating pre-marital intercourse, and so on, while even the actors shrank back. Only a perceptively-aimed question by the company director elicited any response at all, and after nearly an hour of this the audience was allowed to crawl away. Memory may have exaggerated description of this fiasco, but not much.

Of course, handled carefully, questioning can lead to a fruitful discussion. This does depend on experienced intuition, but not entirely; it is possible to work out in advance the kind of question which will be needed with any age group in likely situations, in order to elicit a clear, constructive reply. The younger the child, the more direct, basic and simple the question will need to be; in early stages of any discussion this is wise practice. Gradually, with older children, as the respondents' grasp of the fundamentals becomes surer, the questioning may become more complex, more open-ended or more subjective. Answers must be treated seriously but need not be taken at face value—in verbalising at all, a child is handling a powerful tool over which he has relatively little control. It may be necessary to probe a little, as far as can be done without putting the child at risk of humiliation.

In his account of a programme in which discussion played a vital part,[54] an actor/teacher shows clearly his awareness of the dynamics of discussion, and describes them accurately:

'The greatest problem I personally found with the programme was the waiting. It is difficult because the basic idea of the performance may ignite many reactions, so one must wait till one emerges that is common to all. If the actor/teacher channels the discussion too much or too soon he will lose the children. Having raised a basic question, how long do you wait? The silence could be the children trying to order their ideas in order to articulate them, in which case you must wait until they are ready; or it could be that nothing is happening and the longer you wait the more they dry up. The greatest problem is that often they try and find the "right" answer or the one they think you want. If you question every reply it also has two effects:
1 Having committed themselves they have to work out the logic completely;
2 If they don't get a "pay-off" soon enough they feel there is no answer and lose concentration.

The process of discussion is a problem especially if the children are not protected by a role, as in this programme. But the problem is not avoided by either leading the discussion too much or by withdrawing from it. The discussion worked best when handled with firmness and when the children were asked very direct questions' (David Pammenter).[55]

This programme has already taken a step towards ensuring a valuable exchange of ideas in a discussion by radically changing its structure. The children were split up into small mixed groups each with an actor. In this way the heterogeneous nature of an audience, instead of leading to inhibition, added variety to the argument, because in a small intimate group the individual child felt he dared to try out his ideas, and they would be listened to, perhaps form a significant part of the ongoing argument. Splitting up an audience into small groups, at least to begin with, ensures a much greater proportion of participation, and usually greater commitment. It may not be necessary to have an actor/teacher guiding the groups so long as the purpose of the discussion is clear. It should have some kind of aim: perhaps to try to come to a resolution or solve a problem, and then report back later to a full discussion of all the audience, where the groups' decisions will be compared and contrasted. The purpose may be more specifically connected with the programme, as in *The Ballad of Billy Martin*, where the group discussion time was in order to formulate questions to ask the characters. It may even verge on being an integral part of the programme: in the college programme for antagonistic fourteen-year-old girls mentioned earlier,[45] when the last playlet was stopped in the middle, the girls' disappointment at having their identification broken and their expectations left unfulfilled was harnessed positively to create through discussion their own solutions. The results of this discussion in their turn were not left as a blank finale, but used as a launching pad into the sphere of educational drama, providing the motivation previously lacking in these girls. The girls were asked to explain their solutions, which themselves sparked off interesting comparative discussion, and the actor/teachers offered to act them out. This they slyly started to do very badly, making such a mawkish travesty of the girls' ideas that, exasperated, the girls stepped in with 'No, not like that ... here, let us show you...'; and they ended up acting out several of their endings with obvious enjoyment.

To break for discussion during a programme has the added advantage, if properly structured to avoid bathos, of catching a problem at its starkest, with the audience's attention concentrated on it. *The Emergent Africa Game* used this technique several times to generate a discussion while the audience was in full possession of all the relevant factors it had been given in the argument. What this programme did not do was to use the discussion within the remainder of the programme; though the discussion sections were interesting, they all had to end 'What do you think? Time will tell if you are right', and all the satisfaction the students had was putting a figurative tick or cross by their answer as they watched the plot continue, not on their decision, but towards the preplanned outcome. There was so much, so many elements of satisfaction in this particular programme that it was bound to be successful anyway, but eliciting ideas and then ignoring them to plough one's own furrow is rather self-defeating and potentially demoralising for an audience. Some programmes overcome this by giving a limited choice of decision and then ending with a piece of theatre reflecting the children's decision, one of several prepared to meet all cases. This gives the children the satisfaction of seeing their own ideas tried out, even if they are shown not to work.

Using discussion in this way, which is still more or less extrinsic, because the audience is still being treated as non-participant spectators, does tend to make the programme fragmentary, and sometimes it seems preferable to try and sustain complete emotional commitment, while still preserving the conditions for intellectual examination of the theme or argument. With this end, a number of programmes have shifted the discussion to the beginning, in some form. The bonus this brings of not risking anti-climax at the end is roughly offset by the danger of losing the surprise and weakening the pro-vocative power of the drama itself. One team have several times used the actor/teachers to give a preliminary lesson; each class within the audience is visited by one of the cast (as themselves—the problems of trying to teach in a role as yet unidentified proving too daunting) who introduces a subject and by careful questioning tries to stimulate discussion and thought. In one instance,[56] each actor/teacher took drawings of local demolition work into the classroom to start the children thinking about the virtues of living in different environments, and to try to focus their minds on the needs and wants of a community. The programme that followed was a piece of straight theatre, intended to sum up entertainingly the subject which had been introduced and to give further food for thought. In this particular programme the lightness and fantasy itself did not really highlight anything, as its relevance was not quite close enough for the children to make the transfer from the story back to their lesson theme.

Quite a popular preliminary way of preparing for a difficult programme, or especially a schools' performance of a 'difficult' play, is to hold a 'workshop'. This can be either intended to stimulate thought on themes from the play or to explain some of the tech-niques of interpretation that are used in the production. When these are done as preliminary drama sessions, with one or two members of the company working with a class, perhaps using improvisation or giving the class problems to work out together, they can be very useful and illuminating. All the examples I have seen of a theatre-based session with the whole, large audience have been virtually valueless, except for an occasional few minutes where a group of actors performs a scene in a number of different ways (and the interest this engenders is rather academic, largely for the aficionados). In order to gain and keep the attention of an audience which is not auto-matically committed either to drama (except as an afternoon off school), or to *Hamlet* (except as an examination hurdle), the actors have to play little warming-up games, sometimes very ingenious, and during them invoke the audience's help, or opinions, or suggestions. These, coming from a large, uninvolved audience, are not infrequently likely to be silly, and the actors may feel constrained to play up to this silliness in order to keep the audience entertained. One team, who were experienced and proficient teachers as well as actors, tried to use members of the audience to direct, design and light one scene from *Henry V*, to which this workshop was a preamble, after enacting a lively parody of these jobs.† They put themselves into a dangerous situation, had to use a certain amount of coercion of the half-constrained 'volunteers', and saved themselves by climbing on the back of these students' embarrassment, to the relieved amusement of the rest of the audience. Finally, although over-all the audience quite enjoyed that morning workshop, it added an hour and a half to what was already a concentration span of over three hours; the production itself was sparkling and very sensitively directed at its fifth-year audience, but many of them were wilting long before the end.

The method which has probably proved the most successful way of encouraging, controlling and sustaining intelligent discussion is that of 'role-questioning'. During or after the programme, the audience is invited to talk to the *characters*, to ask them why they did as they did, or to try out on them newly formed opinions of their behaviour. In a way this is more than merely extrinsic; it is inviting the spectators into a direct personal relationship with the characters of the drama, bringing the audience at least to its edge. If the programme has worked its spell properly, the most inhibited of children can feel strongly enough to want to find out why, or to give a character a piece of his mind. The children are still slightly protected in this context by the umbrella of the drama's unreality, and impelled by its glamour; they know that all comments will be received in the safe confines of the play. There is, too, the delight of 'making the skeleton dance' at will. Really progressive dramatic interaction can happen, as the characters are challenged to justify their actions on their own terms. It is undoubtedly very demanding for the actors to maintain their roles strongly in an unscripted and unpredictable dialogue; anti-climax is always at hand, especially if the characters are being questioned one at a time, as in *The Ballad of Billy Martin* where the spectators have been given extra time to marshal their wits and their questions; quite often in this programme the actors sagged out of role as they talked too much, trying to find the right thing to say. To guard against this, some teams prefer to face the audience all together in the discussion, so that they can back each other up if one is flustered or thrown by a question. In the programmes about suicide[28] and schizophrenia[27] mentioned earlier the whole 'family' came out and invited questions. Comment from the audience stimulated improvised arguments among themselves, briefly very entertaining, but occasionally both reams fell into the trap of being carried away by their own roles and holding the stage in what was a weak repetition of the economical theatricality of the programme itself, flattering to the egos of the actors, but deadening to the students' contribution.

One or two brave teams have taken this technique further and stopped the action for the children to discuss the situation with the characters, who then carried on the play according to the advice the children had given them. There are obvious limitations on this method, as a proliferation of possible continuations would mean the abandonment of any structure, but it seems certainly a technique worth exploring in more depth and more frequently; it takes a step further towards integrating the audience's contributions into the experience positively, with results evident, while still preserving very firmly for the children the security of their role as an audience and as nothing more.

Peripheral participation

The most important limiting factor on the degree of participation which can be used is the size of the audience. The closer each child is to the centre of the action and the more he is acted upon, the deeper his involvement. Numbers above sixty very much limit the amount of physical involvement possible (or at least controllable) and in such large groups active planning, decision-making and even speaking are impracticable except for a very few; for those few, as they become conscious of being singled out, such a large passive group is inhibiting not reassuring, and they are bound to be self-conscious—this embarrassment applies even more where there is a physical element than in discussion.

Many companies attempt to use as much participation as possible every time, assuming that, as it is something extra, it must heighten the theatrical experience. In practice, the benefits of a participation which is momentary and superficial may well be outweighed by the disadvantage that it merely arouses a shallow excitement it cannot satisfy, a reaction which destroys the intensity of the children's projection of their imaginative identification by breaking their concentration. The magic *does* get lost.

The simplest and most peripheral participation is a warm-up, where a character, often identifiable as the 'Link' or storyteller, comes and talks to the children, educing simple responses like clapping, or ritual replies; sometimes all the actors go and introduce themselves to a few children each. Since the children are usually excited already, the most valuable function this can have is to calm them down by quietly chatting, rather than bellowing 'I'm Uncle Ted; hello-ello-ello, children!', and waiting for them to bellow back, 'Hello-ello-ello, Uncle Ted!', which just makes it harder for them to concentrate when the play starts. Children become used early in life to the convention of the communal shout or chorus, 'Are you ready now? One, two, three, . . .' so they know they will probably be expected to call out when they go to a show; if it is not over-employed, it probably does little harm to their concentration, though it is usually so drearily predictable that it is difficult to see what possible positive value its exponents think it has to the theatrical experience. If it is given a positive purpose within the plot, for instance when the children are asked to sing a song to disenchant the prince, then it certainly achieves a brief satisfaction. Physical participation on a large audience scale tends to be equally sterile—the hero is going on a sea journey, so the actors throw imaginary ropes to the children and shout at them to pull; the children pull.

Just occasionally this can be made to be more than a meaningless exercise. In a programme about a monster called *The Lambton Worm*[57] the children had been encouraged to react throughout by singing bits of the well-known song that they had previously been taught in preparation, with lots of cries of 'Hello, Harry,' and 'Look out behind you', while a few had helped as extras; although none of this seemed at first to have much point, it had established the idea that the children were *included* (as an audience at a play which was disturbed by a 'real' mystery; their relationship to the 'actors' who were equally surprised by the Pirandellian intrusion was cleverly and disingenuously developed.) During the exciting climax the evil old witch swept out leaving *all* the other characters, including a 'real' policeman, hypnotised in a trance that only a loud whistle would break. Nothing more was said; nobody moved. It was merely a matter of time—a long and intense moment—until the children realised that they, and only they, had the power to release the spell and continue the play; then the barriers of individual inhibition had to be broken as somebody had to venture out on to the acting area, actually touch a character, take the policeman's whistle out of his pocket and blow it. In the slavery programme for juniors,[20] the trick of asking the children physically to sign on as crew for a voyage of adventure which was later revealed as a slaving expedition showed an equally clever use of peripheral participation, though this programme weakened the effect of the coup by meanwhile briefly endowing the children in several other roles, as slaves, townsfolk, the crew of a different ship, at one point two separate roles simultaneously.

Asking for a few volunteers to act as extras (for example, ten to be the Lambton Worm's tail and another dozen to be his victims) can add to the fun, though it does nothing for serious absorption, as the participants are self-conscious, and the rest more interested in them than in what is happening. In a modernised version of *The Pilgrim's Progress*,* † about twenty or thirty volunteers were called out to be the inhabitants of Vanity Fair. The main action and dialogue were pre-planned and sacrosanct, so the actors spent half an hour coaching and rehearsing the extras while the rest watched. The scene was then enacted 'properly'; the potentially very dramatic arrest and trial of Christian, not surprisingly, made little real impact, though both participants and spectators found it all quite fun. Towards the end they were all supposed to chant, 'Let him live . . . Let him live . . .'. In one performance, a sceptical group of boys started chanting, 'Kill him . . . Kill him.' The actors were sensitive enough to realise that, whatever the boys' motives, here was a potential confrontation where the book's exposition of crowd behaviour could dramatically spring to life, but the play had to go on as written, and the moment was lost.

Too often the children's contribution is received negatively, because of the structure of the play. Perhaps in the example above, the actors would invite too much risk if they took up what was, after all, an unsolicited and disaffected contribution. Quite often, though, the children's advice and opinions are solicited, only to be rejected or ignored. This was true in small measure of both the slavery programme and *The Emergent Africa Game*; more seriously true of a play where the children, on a space journey, were offered a direct choice between returning to Earth to save the human inhabitants, including their families, or going on, to a beautiful alluring planet of superbeings who would help them construct a new, happy earth colony.* † This was a well-set-up situation, with the children, through a link character, enabled to ask as many questions as they liked of one of these superbeings, a disembodied voice. After a very intelligent questioning session, bringing out all the factors for and against each alternative, the children were asked to decide, and a vote was taken. By a clear majority in the session I saw, they voted to go on and abandon the Earth to its fate. Astonishingly the voice declared that they could not after all do this, that to go back was the 'right' and moral thing

Trafficking in slaves (*The Story of Jonathan Strong*)

to do, and 'she' was arranging to get them back to Earth. A quick trip back after this admonition, they were perfunctorily dumped back on Earth, and the play was over, leaving many disgruntled children feeling that they had been cheated. I think, too, that a number of youth club members were entitled to feel a little betrayed by the team who prefaced their programme[33] by asking the youngsters various questions about current affairs, or their general outlook on life, then tape-recording the answers. The intention was to evince negative, blank, or ignorant replies, because the start of the programme depended on these being played back to the whole audience with the implied question, 'Are you satisfied with being so ignorant?' The action that followed then had something of the moralistic flavour of a fable. Perhaps I am being too pernickety, though, because the programme was very well received by its audiences, who clearly bore no grudge (and youth club audiences, freed from the restraints of school or theatre, with their five-a-side football curtailed for the programme, are notoriously hard to please).

A common method of participation, invoking very full physical contributions from the children, is used mainly by companies that prefer to call themselves children's theatre teams. It has the advantage of being usable with quite large audiences. In a typical example,* the actors introduce the story (usually well-known, say that of Ulysses), point out to the children how few actors there are, and invite them to help act out the story. They then separate the children into several groups, representing crew-members, the Cyclops's sheep, clashing rocks, and the whirlpool Charybdis, and train them for a few minutes in what to do during 'their scene'. The action is started, and played through with the actors cueing in the children for their parts in each section by simple commands; so, at any point, a few of the children are 'being' the rocks, or the crew, while the rest watch. At first sight the participation, being in a sense total throughout the play, seems integral, but basically it has the same function as in the version of Vanity Fair mentioned above: the structure is unalterable and the children's role is that of extras, merely reacting in a pre-arranged way to the action. There is a great deal of controversy about the value of this kind of participation, controversy that tends to polarise the distinction between children's theatre and theatre in education. When the children's role and reactions are assessed coolly, this question resolves itself logically according to the aims of the company. There is no doubt that, if handled responsibly, young children especially very much enjoy this kind of participation, and they enjoy watching their colleagues performing, too; their desire to be actively involved in any experience is satisfied. To provide this simple lively enjoyment is usually the aim of children's theatre. However, it is less appropriate for theatre in education. For one thing, the storyline has to be kept single and episodic, the theatrical tension very dilute, in order to keep the audience's minds on it, ready to do the right thing at the right time, because the children are likely to be distracted by preoccupation with their share of the action, and by enjoying watching their friends. More important, the level of their commitment to their parts is inevitably very superficial; there is neither time nor point in creating a deep understanding of being a whirlpool or a wind, and really to feel the agonies and excitements of Ulysses's crew takes much more time, different techniques and smaller audiences. The children do what they are told, self-consciously and limply; they are left with a rather fragmented final impression of what is usually inevitably rather a banal story. This is in no way a value judgment on children's theatre; where the aim is lively fun it is achieved. It will not do, however, for theatre in education, where the content must be strong enough to stretch the minds of the audience, the theatricality and participation intense enough to stretch their sensibilities.

Playing games with the children is a popular route to rapport, a destination not always reached. Whether playing Chinese whispers round the room is likely to increase an audience's motivation to identify with the processes of French history, or the characters enacting those processes, is doubtful, though it passes the time amiably enough. In the prototype of a documentary programme about the Trade Unions,[58] playing games actually trivialised the whole approach, most unjustly for the good intentions of the actors, who had slightly misjudged their audience. The programme was designed to use a lot of significant participation, and finish with an entirely participatory simulation game, so to try and break through the inhibitions of the audience, who had an age range of fifteen to eighteen and came from two different schools, the team started by playing a few simple warming-up games, of the kind often used by actors, theatre workshops and educational drama teachers; ingeniously but too tenuously they tried to relate them to the concept of working together in a common conflict (solidarity and the Trade Union movement). A group of sixth-form boys, unused to drama in education and uncommitted to theatre, resented them as 'kids' games', beneath their dignity, and ostentatiously showed their scorn. This attitude was sycophantically taken up by some fifth-year girls eager to impress, and although the actor/teachers worked very hard, eventually recapturing some measure of interested acceptance, both theatricality and involvement were badly shaken. It might be said that this behaviour was the result of variables over which the team had no control, but, even so, by happening it showed up the weaknesses of this type of participation, especially with senior students—after all, these variables are common enough. The team thought so, too, and shortened the whole first half, tightening up the theatricality, with much more success.

If games are to be used, they really need a more vital or integral function in the drama; later in the same programme, the students were invited to play 'historical Bingo', the endless repetitiousness of vital but meaningless dates being humorously echoed by the compulsive monotony of the game; this Bingo session was then made the framework holding a number of historical sketches, each depicting a significant historical event in the development of Trade Unionism. The students saw the point of the exercise and took part much more willingly.

On the whole, though, playing games together is a much more natural activity for young children, and it is with juniors that the technique works best. Games were used very cunningly in the Welsh language programme *Syrca Sulwen*; though they had little to do with the dramatic process, the word and movement games the children played had everything to do with the educational purpose, and were given a natural context in a circus environment, where the children could accept the idea of clowns wanting to play games with children as quite credible.

A rare, very successful and totally integrated use of games with older students comes in *Snap out of It* where the adaptation of actors' trust exercises with blindfolds, complemented by powerful readings about madness, carried within its experience the whole message of the programme, which the preliminary 'theatre' spectacle apparently belied. This really raised these exercises into the category of integral participation.

The most successful and nicely judged use of purely peripheral participation I have seen was in a programme taking place in a theatre with an audience of four hundred.[59] The children were ushered to their seats by immaculate 'stewardesses', and each given a ticket for a hovercraft cruise to the North Pole. The whole auditorium was turned into a hovercraft 'set'. During the performance the children, consistently endowed as child tourists on a schools' cruise, were often directly talked to, or appealed to (in a structured way, ensuring the right response); they had to explain things, act as lookouts issuing warnings, and practise safety procedures. There was a (well-disguised and motivated) lesson on how a hovercraft works, with the opportunity to ask questions. Some boxes, casually passed back by the children to be stacked at the start, were later revealed to be full of nitro-glycerine, and at a very tense moment the children had to unpack and pass the nitro down to the front, with fear and trembling. There was plenty of action and excitement to keep them absorbed in the plot even as they took part, and any tendency to excited over-reaction was expertly dealt with.

Stimulating as this was, and I think it increased the children's absorption and enjoyment (certainly judging by their reactions during the programme and in the interval), the quality of the experience was still primarily theatrical. The structure of the play was clearly defined throughout, and the children's contribution could not affect it (even if the nitro had been dropped, it would not have exploded then but would still have had to when needed!). In their roles as sightseers the children were acted upon superficially, asked to react in non-crucial contexts, but took no part in the development of the drama.

Integral participation

For this, small audiences are essential, small enough for the actors to control the participation sufficiently closely for the focus to be kept clearly on the central drama at all times; and for children's individual or small group contributions to be registered, considered and sometimes acted upon.

Both these needs become more difficult to achieve with numbers above about forty, virtually impossible above sixty (though Coventry did achieve them once with a heavily structured simulation game about slavery), so programmes aiming at integral participation usually work with one class of children, or at most two. There is another reason for this, too—the participation element often demands a high level of co-operative activity; as the actors cannot instantly create this, it is usually preferable to have a class that is used to working together. It is possible to exploit the dynamics of the class for the programme's ends; the natural rivalry between two parallel classes can be harnessed in their endowment as opposing forces in a documentary conflict (say, one class as Roundheads, the other as Cavaliers, or one as striking pitmen, the other as blacklegging candymen). In the programme *Ghost in the Village*, the original proposal to do this in order to further the rivalries between the villages of Thockrington and Bavington was eventually rejected in favour of its obverse; deliberately splitting up real friendship groups from within the one class would create more telling moral and emotional tensions when the issues of personal survival and mutual aid were being decided.

Age is another important factor. Children between about seven and eleven will willingly throw themselves into anything offered that looks exciting—the more directly they are involved, the better. In their own games they are used to exhibiting and projecting their identification with dramatic characters quite freely and unselfconsciously in public. They are accordingly the easiest age groups to organise into situations of total participation such as have already been described.

Below seven, great care must be taken, as the children's sociability and their security are much more fragile; new situations are as fraught with danger as with excitement, hence the games the Chamberlain plays in *The Happy Land*. Hence, too, the importance of having the Chamberlain. With young children the Link character is more than the narrator, or the one who organises what is going to happen next. He is the yardstick by which the fantasy can be judged, his reactions give them the security to know how they ought to react, and, having brought them into the fantasy, he can presumably take them out if the experience becomes too much. So the team who chose a friendly witch as their Link deprived the children of the Link's most important function, and they paid for it.

Above eleven or so, full participation becomes more and more difficult as self-esteem becomes all-important, conformity and caution the protection of that self-esteem, and fantasy is rejected in favour of recognisable 'reality'; asking an adolescent to exhibit an emotional reaction and act on that rather than upon his convention is asking him to risk both self-esteem and that of his peers. He turns his back on 'let's pretend' and will only assume personae that he can accept as real. (This is a generalisation; there are, of course, exceptions.) So either fraudulent ruses have to be played in programmes for adolescents (as one was on the girls who had no time for school or drama), or some new approach has to be found.

The most popular alternative is the straight simulation game, where it is made clear that the students are representing an interest, and a novel perspective on reality will emerge if they are willing to act a part essential for the mechanics of the exercise.

'In all simulations players take on roles *which are representative of the real world* ... the participant must merely accept a new identity ... the essential core is understanding the situation of another person, and feeling it emotionally' (J. Taylor and R. Walford).[60]

So long as this is made clear beforehand, then the situation becomes safely objective and the students can participate without inhibition. They then often develop subjective emotional identification with their role just as strong as juniors endowed with fictional roles. A typical use of simulation with sixth formers (very similar in structure to the Trade Union programme) was developed out of the junior programme about the run-down of London Docks, by the same company. Called *What do you do when the Docks ain't Docks*,[61] it started with a theatrical montage of songs and sketches, accompanied by carefully chosen slides illustrating the whole history of London Docks, and particularly their effect on the dockland community. In the afternoon the students were shown, with the aid of more slides and an overhead projector, a simulated model area of dockland, designated for redevelopment. They were then split into small groups, and each group was assigned an interest in the development (among those represented were local residents, property developers, industrialists, London Transport, conservationists, and so on). They all set to with enthusiasm to design their ideal schemes, listen to others' opposing interests and consider various kinds of compromise, firstly preselected, then selected by one of the groups acting as a committee. Some measure of absorption was sustained right until the end, though by then the structure of the simulation had rather diffused it and blurred some of the central issues in a way which highlights the main problem which TIE teams face in incorporating simulations into their programmes. To begin with, the actors were forced to drop out of role (organising a simulation is a teaching job) and it seemed a pity, after generating a good deal of theatrical energy, just to let it peter out in what is, in terms of spectacle, bound to be repetitious. The teaching itself was then diffused among the actors, who were all trying to assist, when it needed to be focused on the one director of the operation; the 'spares' hovering about half-in, half-out of role, would have done better to have gone home. There were certainly moments of real drama developed between the groups as interests clashed, but these grew fewer and weaker as the repetitive demands of the progression of the simulation had to be met. This programme cried out for a final, theatrical climax; at the end, after a useful and quite stimulating discussion, there was a definite sense of 'end of the lesson' as the students filed out; they were not at all antagonistic, but the feeling was clearly perceptible. The theatricality was dead, relegated to the minor servicing function of being a starter to stimulate interest in a very good and well-prepared lesson; it left me wondering again about those words: '. . . it seems a pity if children have to be everlastingly educated, in the name of theatre'.

Surely it is not only possible but entirely desirable to keep alive the element of theatre in simulation work, rather than just to present it baldly. To use actors in role as integral parts of the simulation, with a range of behaviour in accordance with those roles, of which the students must take account, could make the whole experience far more intrinsically exciting. In particular, if within that range they act unpredictably, this would add the element of chance which educationists recognise as desirable in simulations, and which at the moment often has to be rather lamely represented by throwing dice. Some TIE simulations have tried to maintain some form of role-play, but it is an area still very under-developed, with the structure demanded by the theatricality too often in conflict with the flexibility needed in the simulation.

At the moment, totally integrated participation is still proving most successful with the age group seven to eleven, several examples of which have been extensively referred to. The success of this type of work depends very largely on the degree to which the audience can be made to feel an important part of the process. Sometimes it is thought that participation would be nice, but the children must not get in the way of the action, so they are given a vague role disguising the fact that they are bystanders, and they trail round after the actors or stand about, like a ragged chorus, doing what they are told. This is not integral participation. What is also bound to get a superficial response is to endow the children with a role towards which they have a stereotyped attitude or of which they have no concept at all, then provide no links: to endow children as Red Indians, or animals in a zoo, and expect them immediately to behave as such, is inviting silliness, not real involvement.

Firstly, it cannot be overstressed that in participation drama, though children may be given roles, they should *never* be expected to 'act'. Participating is not the same thing as performing; to act out is a natural, unselfconscious activity, to act a part is artificial and deliberate. This is not to suggest that children do not enjoy performing, or should never be given a chance to do this, but rather that it is utterly inappropriate in a context where the children's experience is exploratory and receptive. The theatricality belongs to the actors and the children must be free to respond naturally within the environment of the drama (that is, their role). Only then can they discover the *truth* about human behaviour that lies behind the dramatic fiction; if they are consciously 'acting' the symbol remains a fantasy that they have created with the judgment of others in mind, and the message is spurious.

I have used the word 'endowment' several times to describe the degree of characterisation which the audience will accept to define their place in the drama. Where the children *are* involved in the action itself there are several different categories of endowment, each of which demands a distinct kind of effort and projection, giving a different total perspective.

First, they can take part as themselves, which is the easiest way to avoid the danger of the children 'acting' (for example, in *The Happy Land*). In a programme like this, the children are swept up into the adventure, and none of them thought it inappropriate when, in answer to the Toymaker's question,

'Where are you all now?', the little girl on the telephone replied,
'The Princess's garden, Newbottle Infants School.'

The younger the children, the more important it is to leave them as themselves; the experience of a six- or seven-year-old is so limited and his ability to identify with what he sees so involuntary that any role demanding a degree of imaginative projection of this identification is too difficult, and his only recourses are rejecting, ignoring the role, or trying to invent something that might fit. There may perhaps be a danger even in leaving the children as themselves. In plays with a high content of fear or tension, role is a protection. If young children are not given a role that reminds them, at moments of crisis, that it is only a play, the more credulous children can be really insecure and frightened, since belief and disbelief are so close, and identification with the action so complete. A dragon frightening the people of Novgorod is one thing, a dragon coming in our school and frightening us is quite another.

As children grow older and more practised in their dramatic play, they gain more control over their ability to project, and can accept role more easily; this is the second category. The simplest kind of endowment is where it is clear to the children that they can fulfil the role quite appropriately just by being themselves—that is, being endowed as children within the story: the children of the village in *The Day of Fire*, or the inhabitants of an orphanage (or, with older children, the careers class in *The Ballad of Billy Martin*). In situations like this, the children may need a little help to project, to find out what is appropriate to the context; although the 'village' children learn like all children, their lessons are in hunting and curing snake-bite. It needs to be emphasised, or kept very clear, that they are still children.

When children are taken a stage further, and finally asked to make the bigger jump to identify with and become people whom they are not, they need more help. It is still possible for them to react naturally, but their scope of action must be more clearly defined. None of the children can imagine really what it feels like to be an unskilled car worker, or a Yorkshire weaver; what the programme can do is to create a standpoint where the children can realise what they have in common with such people, and understand concretely some aspect of their lives. Then a really deep endowment is possible. Two techniques have proved invaluable here: relating to jobs and families, and introducing occupational mime.

To take jobs and families first: Yorkshire weavers lived in families which did jobs; modern children live in families doing jobs, and they understand already how families operate. So a useful first step towards endowment might be to split the children into small groups as families, with relationships they can work out themselves. Gradually information and controls can be fed in by subtle theatricality of the actor/teachers; the vicar might call and by his expectations, expressed in the cues he gives, make clear the relationship the villagers have with the church and the gentry; a conflict of interest, expressed in a staged confrontation between an independent weaver and a mill owner, can introduce the drama itself as well as filling out the dramatic background for the children. Because it clearly relates to their own experience, as well as offering a new experience, the children will enjoy it and become very involved; it satisfies those two basic requirements of *recognition* and *curiosity*.

The children will still react in their own way; they may even use external factors from what they have observed to help them. In doing this, they may well start acting; it is justifiable for a child playing a grandmother to use a stick as a property to help her feel the role more; if she then develops what she conceives to be an appropriate tottering gait and shaking hand it means she is not involved in her role herself, but performing it for the benefit of others—the quickest way to scotch this reaction is to keep the children too busily occupied to have time for self-regard. Therefore, actors should never expect a child to try and behave like an old woman; her role should be given limitations strong and clear enough for her to behave naturally, and this will be appropriate to the behaviour of *that* particular old woman in *that* circumstance. Some of the children may react entirely sincerely in a way which the actor/teachers know to be inappropriate, perhaps because in the improvisation a situation has arisen which is not covered by their code of reference. Wherever possible the actors should accept these *faux pas*, and direct them into a different direction or play them down; if a contribution, offered genuinely, has to be rejected out of hand, then this must still be done within the pretexts provided by the drama:

'No, I don't think you should rush off now and kill the dragon with your bare hands —yes, I know you're very strong, but we need your strength too much to risk your getting killed.'

It is not difficult to give the children's activity a purpose that is meaningful to them so that they can feel that by their involvement the drama is progressing. A sheep-shearing festival will be fun, it will need preparation, and the jobs entailed in that preparation are recognisable, though some of them may be new.

This brings us to the second standby for speedy endowment: occupational mime. The same principles apply; to give the children an interesting activity which they can recognise as purposeful, and which needs concentration. Activity in itself is fun, so being taught how to fire a musket and wield a cutlass (quite glamorous skills in themselves) have certainly enough initial motivation to keep the children working hard while the deeper understanding of why they might need to fire a musket and chop the heads off the evil Roundheads/Cavaliers is being fed in. It is both interesting and narrowly educational for the children to learn-by-doing exactly how a handloom works (especially if they are given a replica to copy their actions from); more important, it can give a crucial glimpse of the repetitive and intensely physical nature of a weaver's life, pinning down one of the central dramatic motives of the programme to a concrete, comprehensible detail. It is not necessary to have thirty handlooms or muskets to practise on; the children are quite used to miming or adapting improbable properties in their own play, and if their interest has been caught they will unselfconsciously drop into this convention.

This kind of role-play needs absolute sincerity to generate belief. The actor/teachers must show through the quality of their role-playing that they are totally committed to the situation. Their acting must be crisp, clear and economical. Any drop into teacherliness leaves the context blurred and the children's belief superficial. The harder the children are worked, the deeper will be the involvement. The Civil War sergeants can order the children about, bully them, rail at them and ruthlessly condemn indifferent or sloppy mime, and the children, completely cushioned by the drama from humiliation or resentment, will respond enthusiastically—after all, it is part of the accepted stereo-type of an army sergeant to bully his recruits; it would not be believable if he did not. In *The Day of Fire*, it is less the characterisation than the plot that provides the motivation for the villagers to spur on the children: if they do not learn properly ('. . . better than that; do it again and put your shoulders into it this time') they will not pass the Chief's initiation test and the ceremony cannot take place. However, plot motivation cannot carry all; relying on these pressures, the actor/teachers in this programme often let their roles sag, with a consequent drop in commitment.

These methods are often time-consuming, but if they are not used, the participation tends to be much more superficial. Two programmes ended with a trial scene, where the children, aided by the actors, had to establish a character's responsibility for a disaster. In one of them,[39] the children had been through the experience of developing family ties and loyalties, working for and defending them, then seeing all they had worked for destroyed—or achieved, depending which side they were on. The argument was always passionate and totally convincing, reaching astonishing depths of under-standing of consequences, as the children challenged each other's outlook or fought for their own. That their final answer was sometimes historically inaccurate did not matter, it was always right for them, and history could be put right in a moment afterwards, sparking off another interesting discussion. In the other programme,[5] a short piece of bustling mime involving putting out the Great Fire of London, where their endowment as citizens was only loosely implied, was the children's only contact with the issue—who started the fire? The defendant was only introduced later, at his trial (historically accurate, but it meant the children had not had time to form an attitude to him, or even to find out who he was). The trial started with a new round of

Bullying is part of the fun (*The Bolton Massacre*)

endowments—court officials, citizens of Pudding Lane, and so on—and witnesses were called. When asked a question like, 'What were you doing in Pudding Lane that morning?', the children had to answer with the first thing that came into their heads, or stand bemused until they were 'helped': 'Were you doing your shopping at the market in Pudding Lane?' The actors worked very hard and very sensitively to establish atmosphere or an understanding of the situation. Sometimes the children were experienced enough in drama, or imaginative enough, to create a strong atmosphere and confident interaction, but usually this was patchy; on at least one occasion with very inhibited children the scene collapsed like a failed cake—something that should not happen to a courtroom drama! Even when it worked well, and it was usually, on its own terms, a successful programme, there was neither the intensity of commitment nor the depth of perception that the other programme achieved.

To appreciate the depth and power of belief which these techniques of total participation, well used, can engender, it is necessary only to see the sustained intensity which the children will put into those areas where they have freedom to respond how they will, and watch their unshakable determination to resolve the hardest dilemma, as well as their imaginative command of all the factors which may be relevant. There is no question that the total experience is an enormously powerful one, by no means inferior to a 'purely' theatrical one, and its intensity remains with the children for a long time. I revisited the class of children three weeks after a performance of one of these programmes when the audience participated fully throughout, and the theatre element, strong in itself, was relegated to a servicing function. I wanted to find out what, if anything, had stuck. They *all* had total recall down to the minutest details of every moment; perhaps more significant was that they had had the experience overlaid by a performance (by a competent company) of a play which was more or less traditionally theatrical, two days before my visit. This some of them already had some difficulty remembering clearly. They had no doubts at all, were completely unanimous, about which of the two they themselves felt to have been the more exciting, memorable and educative session.

Chapter Six

Contents and contexts

The age barrier 'Almost any material can be taught honestly to a child of any age' (Jerome Bruner).[62]

Seven of the speakers at a recent national conference entitled 'Writing for Young People's Theatre' quite independently made the statement, 'We mustn't talk down to children'. None of them tried to expand upon it much or challenge it, and they all quickly moved on to the richer fields of selling plays and using well-known fairy-tales; one speaker, it is true, did briefly illustrate it by declaring a political intent in an anthropomorphic fable he had written. In the main, however, the words seemed more of a pious gesture, a ritual incantation, than anything else. I think the statement, in so far as it is capable of definition, is extremely misleading—as misleading, out of a specific context, as the Bruner quotation heading this chapter (also quoted out of context) with which it may seem synonymous. Both are a useful warning against patronising and underestimating children by giving them trivial or inconsequential subject-matter; no more than that. It should be noted that Bruner was talking specifically about the cognitive sphere of learning, and mainly about information processing; TIE makes its impact at least equally on other areas of a child's receptivity. While it is certainly true that it is hard to overestimate the capacity of children to comprehend simple subject matter presented sincerely, it is nonsense to pretend that the differences in emotional, social and intellectual development of differing age groups are not absolutely crucial to the presentation of that subject matter—a truism to all those in direct contact with children, not always so clearly understood in children's theatre.

By preparing its own material TIE has a great opportunity; it can present its subject matter in a way exactly tailored to the needs of particular ages and types of children, ensuring that their capacities are fully stretched without them being bored or un-warrantably frightened. Any TIE programme or children's play that intends or pretends to appeal to a wide age range risks some kind of negative response for at least some of the time.

'A theatrical performance requires an audience to identify with what is happening on stage. Identification cannot take place unless:
1 an audience member is predisposed to identify;
2 he has ability to empathise;
3 he has experience to draw on in order to put what is happening on stage in a personal context;
4 he has sufficient intellectual grasp of the subject matter to filter his own emotional response;
5 he has sufficient stability to come to terms with the emotional experience on reflection.
If a child lacks 1, 2, or 3, he is going to be bored by the experience. If he lacks 4, what he understands through his emotions only may be distressing for him, and if he has all four qualities except the last he may well have nightmares' (Gavin Bolton).[63]

One might add to this that if a child feels that the material is beneath him, that he is being patronised because what he sees presents no challenge to his abilities 2 to 5, then he will *not* be predisposed to identify.

Within the narrowest age range there will be diversities of individual reaction, according to each child's emotional and intellectual maturity, and of group reaction, according to the sophistication of the children's expectations. The programme needs to be flexible enough to enable it to be tuned to the wavelength of the class, and to enable children to make different levels of response or contribution within it. The actors need great sensitivity to group and individual feedback in order to tune it precisely, and also ensure that all contributions are positive, whatever their level. To take a few examples: an audience of articulate, middle-class children, their minds enriched with stories at home and at school, and used to the conventions of educational drama, will be confident, capable of self-control and self-direction, but very demanding of challenging material, and ready to withhold their belief. Children whose culture is not primarily verbal, and whose minds are not dulled by constant exposure to powerful dramatic symbols, will identify much more easily and involuntarily with a programme, and need a gentler, slower approach. Lively children, used to being inhibited and totally directed in school, may want to employ the programme as an escape valve and may not understand the internal controls of drama, so they will need very firm, even ruthless handling. Disturbed children will be easily frightened, and so on.

This variety of response applies particularly, though not solely, to participation work. In *The Happy Land* the Wizard spends the first few minutes sitting in his hideout trying to gauge the level of the children, because his first entrance is crucial: when he appears, they must be scared of him, just scared enough to believe in what he has done to the Princess; to be determined to help the Princess to overcome his power; not to dare to approach him. Stealing back the keys is then an appropriately nerve-racking experience, and the children's power of decision over him at the end a very satisfying reversal. If the Wizard misjudges his first entrance by overplaying it, the more nervous children can run screaming through the door, or dissolve in tears on their teacher's lap. If he under-plays it, the children will want to be all over his den, mauling him about to show that they are not afraid. All three of these reactions have happened with children in the single range six-plus to seven-minus years old. The actor/teachers' job becomes harder when working in vertically grouped and all-age schools, with the children some years apart in age. This problem has to be faced another way in secondary schools, where the enormous gap between the emotional maturation of boys and girls often seems almost unbridgeable, their preoccupations, likes and defences are so different. It is possible when the children are working more or less on their own, as in the infants' programme exploring the qualities of a net,[64] and in presentation drama, where the response is also primarily individual, to cater for a larger age range, because up to a point each child can draw from the total experience at his own level. Integral participation demanding collaborative input and group responses eventually becomes impossible or meaningless.

Axioms and clichés

'There is a terrible sameness about plays for young children,' said a bored teacher. 'They're all JAM—Journeys, Animals and Magic. I'd like a bit more meat for my kids.' Even in TIE's short life, some of the conventions which started off as ingenious ideas, or were already standard fittings in children's drama, seem to be becoming ritualised into dogma, security symbols perhaps necessary for inexperienced teams to build on, but often accepted without thought. They need re-examination (though not necessarily rejection).

Starting with fundamentals, there can be very little doubt that strength of storyline is very important for young children. Through stories children's understanding is both widened and pulled into coherent shape. Eric Bentley, describing 'Story' as 'halfway house between Life and Plot',[65] defines the process of story as satisfying the demands of *sequence*, *causality* and *selectivity*. A young child's life is a welter of impressions, many of which make no sense; some are frightening, others may not be trustworthy—but which? It is so difficult to tell what matters and what does not. In a story, a child experiences a series of events, which he can see are linked together; he can understand from this model not only *that* (*b*) follows (*a*), but *why* it does. He is also freed from having to pick the relevant data out from the general jumble; they are selected for him. As he grows older, the sequence can be more complex, and as other dimensions appear, the importance of storyline diminishes.

What about fantasy? It is regarded as an integral part of most young children's stories, as it is obviously an integral part of their lives. It is not a static ingredient, though, but an operative process; through fantasy children (and adults too) purge themselves of anxiety about desires which they know to be wrong or socially unacceptable; they externalise and so start to come to terms with deep fears; they relieve frustrations by solving problems through wish-fulfilment. Their use of fantasy helps to give them a yardstick to measure what is real or acceptable by defining what is not:

'The more Caroline's fantasies became violent and uncontrolled, the more controlled her real behaviour became and the more sense of reality she showed' (A. Davidson and J. Fay).[66]

Fantasies have a high dramatic content, for they express conflicts in symbolic terms, and (in normal children) are acted out in safe, consequence-free environments: the child's thoughts, the stories he tells, reads or is told, and his play. The fantasies interact with reality both ways—they are modified by the demands of sharing fantasies in storytelling or communal play; they then feed back into the child's understanding of the real world.

The deliberate invocation of fantasy images, channelled and modified in story and drama, can intensify this feedback.

This whole interaction is a powerful process, which demands and has always demanded potent symbols. In a discussion among a group of teachers about what story material concerning social problems is suitable for young people, an example for consideration described in detail a particularly unpleasant case of baby battering, where the father, a man of diminished responsibility and quick, ungovernable temper, had been left alone to look after the baby, while his wife was out; the child's persistent screaming, which he was powerless to stop, preyed on his nerves until, not knowing what he was doing, he suddenly attacked the baby, killing it. When his wife returned, and, weeping, bitterly upbraided him, he then turned, distraught, on her and killed her too—and so on. Most of the teachers declared firmly that this subject was not suitable for children under sixteen, in any form, no matter what distancing convention was used; it was too frightening, meddling in terrors and aggressions not really understood. It was, of course, the story of *Punch and Judy* which was being described, that most durable and archetypal cathartic fantasy story. The same week as that discussion, a friend had heard some children playing a singing game, starting with the words,

> 'Mary Ann Cotton, she's dead and she's rotten,
> She lies in her grave and her eyes are wide open...'

which referred to a local multiple murderess, notorious a hundred years ago, whom adult history preferred to forget, but whose story has proved quite lasting in this children's song, which goes on to even more gruesome details.

Obviously, when tapping for TIE such potent instincts, enormous care and sensitivity are needed, both in preparation and in performance, but that is no excuse for shirking the responsibility. At the worst, children are remarkably resilient. One TIE team leader maintained that in their infant school programme they had attempted to give the children an experience which was enjoyable, and where they could feel *entirely safe throughout*.† The result was a spineless little story, radiating genteel goodwill, where each problem as it came up was solved instantly, usually by magic, and there was no villain. The children's attention was just about held by the very competent acting and attractive costumes, but it was difficult to see what the team could imagine was educative about it. I later discovered that their method of preparing a story was for the leader to give the team five random and unrelated ideas, then three minutes to make up a story together, using all these five items. This story was then scripted and produced just as it was; little wonder it was too feeble and simplistic for the purpose of fantasy to operate on even the lowest level. Such a story, though prepared with the best of intentions, can be no more than an insult to children's intelligence and buoyancy. As the article by Gavin Bolton quoted earlier in this chapter continues: 'If a show guarantees that children's emotional level remains at low ebb in the name of safety, they might as well have stayed at home.'[63]

Some symbols seem to hold their power, no matter how familiar, a fact that many teams trade on, doing their best to devalue them by over-use; among these, princesses, witches and wizards, dragons, clowns and toys that come to life rank high in the ratings, along with the ubiquitous animals that can talk. It is perhaps perfectly reasonable to use these universally popular elements, providing that the programme does not hang too much of its effect on them—in other words, providing it can offer something new. *The Princess, the Sweep and the Pedlar* brought these tired characters together in an imaginative context that very much intrigued the children. In an anthropomorphic programme, *How do you swim on Concrete?*,[67] the children meet a stupid duck, a pompous frog and a sharp-talking squirrel who all live by a pond; this programme slides no further into empty fable, however, because the children have to help the animals save their houses from a greedy property developer (more of a cliché for adults!), and finally to decide between keeping their pond or having a children's playground there instead, and solve the problems posed by whichever they choose.

Good young children's programmes, even if they use fantasy figures, eschew too-easy solutions; magic in particular is more often than not a fraud, cheating the children of a testing and logically satisfying ending, something the team were well aware of in this account of an infant programme:

'*Gremian* is a fantasy story about the last few Gremians to survive the long war with the Burks—parasites that are almost blind and need to attach themselves to the hands of the Gremians who are then forced to take them to their food, rubbish. The Gremians are trying to clear all the rubbish from the beaches, old train tunnels and rubbish dumps, etc., and travel about in their "dormi". During the story the children help the Gremians to overcome the Burks and their leader. They are successful and the story ends happily. The story was a good example of logical fantasy, never taking advantage of the children's inexperience and never having to introduce magic to untie the knots in the plot. The "dormi" was an important feature of the programme. It was brightly coloured with doors and windows, and when the children were inside sound effects and bright lights helped to create the illusion of journeying. The Burks were puppets, and as well as being seen fixed to an unfortunate Gremian's hand they could be heard scratching on the outside of the dormi or seen framed in the open window—like a puppet show.

For some children the programme was quite frightening but if they channelled their anxieties into activity and discussion with the Gremians they would live through the experience to the happy ending' (Bolton Theatre in Education).[68]

This account also refers to two of the other standbys of infant drama: happy endings and journeys. It brings out the genuine importance of the happy ending at this age; not only must the story have a completeness that satisfies the child's need for causality and sequence—allowing him to perceive a wholeness in the pattern—but if the programme has been truly challenging it will have aroused strong emotional tensions (in this case, genuine fear) which need to be set at rest; no residue of worry must be left. In an early performance of *The Happy Land*, the children suggested killing the Wizard; anxious to respond honestly to the children's ideas, the company, who in this eventuality had briefed the Toymaker to take the Wizard away for execution, agreed. Before they could act on it, a dominant child picked up a magic (invisible) dagger and gleefully ran it through the Wizard, who had no option but to collapse there and then. The final 'happy' dance took place round this macabre sprawled black carcase, to the obvious anxiety of some of the children. Since then, killing the Wizard has always been rejected, and the children have been forced to work for some positive resolution.

Journeys, however, though very useful ways of keeping the story moving (literally) are not, as some people seem to think, part of the regulations for young children's theatre. They can be rather empty, repetitive affairs, if they lack imagination. It is possible to have a programme which does not involve the children in going anywhere: in one clever programme the children were all zipped inside a tent for most of the performance as they braved the rigours of an arctic winter. In what have become known as 'Adventure' programmes, the school itself is the environment, and the action intrudes

Nervously entering the 'dormi' (*Gremian*)

on the ordinary school day. There is a knock on the door of the classroom, and a
'workman' appears carrying a parcel. He has come to mend the pipes, he says; after
a few disruptive minutes he goes away to fetch another tool, leaving the parcel. While
he is away another workman comes in, also to mend the pipes, and becomes excited
when he hears of his predecessor, who, it seems, is a fraud. All is not as it appears,
and what is in the parcel? The children are caught up in a mystery of spies and secrets,
which they help to solve; realisation that they are in a play dawns only gradually, for
they are still in the classroom, still themselves.

If magic and unreality are used, the Songman programme results (see Appendix,
pages 146–58) suggest that the illusion needs to be complete, judging by the children's
more superficial involvement when they could see the tape recorder. This does not apply
to older children, and magic is only really usable at all with under-eights; above that
age, the children start becoming sceptical. Much of the initial interest in illusion is
in seeing how it works, which is obviously a distraction from the purpose of the illusion
in the programme; once an understanding has been established children can accept
it entirely and adopt it into the framework of their suspension of disbelief. The unconscious selectivity of nine- or ten-year-olds is quite well enough developed, largely through
their own play where they are in and out of role all the time, for them to ignore what
is not relevant to the experience with which they choose to identify, provided they are
not distracted by their curiosity. This makes me doubt the validity of these challenging
words:

> 'I have noticed actors in Theatre for Children groups walk off an arena area and
> while still in sight relax and come right out of character. This of course destroys
> credibility for the child: it becomes just vague fun instead of the emotional and
> aesthetic experience it should be ... sometimes just bewildering. Don't be led away
> by suspension of belief, disbelief, cynical unsuspension and all that. If people want
> any audiences for the future they had better leave incredulity alone. The only way
> is to provide what the children can understand as the truth' (Peter Slade).[69]

This seems to me to underestimate the children. Most TIE companies give children
more credit, make no attempt to hide the fact that they are actors, and few concessions
towards naturalism. Certainly a casual or sloppy approach to the conventions of the
play can destroy the involvement. If these conventions are clearly defined, the children

can respond appropriately: *The Day of Fire* demanded a continuous deep involvement in a very alien, fictitious environment; both sound and lighting effects were used to heighten the atmosphere and help the children to identify, and the technicians, lighting panel, tape recorder and other sound effects were clearly visible throughout. Having registered them, right at the beginning, the children always *completely* ignored them, and also any adult observers, up to thirty-five in number, sitting unobtrusively. It is the power of the acting, and the intensity of the theatricality itself, that define the conventions for the children, and these will dictate the depth of their belief, not the presence or absence of external distraction. It is usually quite possible to define exactly the conventions *within* the drama itself. Occasionally it is necessary, and the children respect this, to invoke their conscious will, as in the rather clumsy controlling technique introducing Part 5 of *Ghost in the Village*, where an actor reappears as himself and asks the children to play a game by his rules.

Controls are of course very important, especially in participation drama. In *Ghost in the Village*, the afternoon session originally started with the Spirit of Cholera rising to make his announcement. The half-frightened, half-amused desire to run away from the lethal 'touch' was far too strong to resist, even for the adults on whom the programme was first tried out, so a totally inappropriate game of 'Tag' developed. Admitting the weakness of their structure, the actor/teachers built in the extra-theatrical appeal to the children to assert conscious self-control.

The easiest form of control, a useful but clumsy device which illustrates audiences' ability to identify at will, is to have a narrator. In younger children's work his role is usually an extension of the Link figure, still providing security as he guides them through the story, with comment, comparison and explanation. At secondary level he can serve the additional purpose of directing the audience's sympathies in four principal ways.

First, he can be neutral, and show up all the factors in turn, or in a two-way drama alternately point out one side of the argument, then the other.

Second, he can be sympathetic and committed to one position in the drama, inviting the audience to share his sympathies, like the 'psychiatrist' in *The Cullen Family*; the danger of this is that, carrying the message of the play in this way, if the students for any reason fail to identify with him, the message too will be rejected.

Third, he can deliberately and provocatively represent the other point of view. *Sweetie*

Pie,[70] a programme making a plea for women to have an equal place with men in society, uses a narrator who represents patronising male chauvinism. The danger here is the converse, that some of the audience will identify with the narrator, who is voicing their preconceptions, and look no further.

Fourth, he can act as a central static point, a measure of the audience's shifting sympathies; in the programme about battered babies, the scrupulous neutrality of the social worker pulled the audience round from sheer hostility to sympathy for the protagonists, then a much more crucial appraisal of all the characters, including the social worker/narrator herself, discovered perhaps to have been wanting in courage.

In their struggle to escape from episodic naturalism and chronological storytelling, in order to give older children a less simplistic experience, TIE teams are busy developing their own, brand-new clichés. To juxtapose a serious problem or plight with parody or grotesque comedy in order to create an ironic understanding is certainly a powerful technique, but one which is being done to death; at times it seems as if behind every serious dramatic moment enacted there lurks a music-hall/circus/television quiz game/ soap opera/advertisement/pub-entertainment waiting to offer its anti-sentimental alienation contribution. *The Ballad of Billy Martin* suffers from this propensity more than most. This technique of ironic reversal shares a disadvantage with the collage structure in which it is often placed in secondary school programmes. It is easy to make the conflict too rarefied or sublimated so that no idea or situation is sustained long enough to build up enough dramatic suspense or atmosphere. The result may be full of secondary theatre, but not necessarily truly dramatic. On the other hand, it is worth bearing in mind, in the ceaseless search for new forms, that what is a cliché to the actor/teachers or adults is not necessarily a cliché to the young people, and this applies to content, too—originally, like relevance, is in the eye of the beholder. Moreover, some clichés, like the well-known stereotyped character, can be a useful form of shorthand, if handled carefully.

There is a movement in TIE that takes its rejection of trivia and inconsequence to great lengths. A programme is not worth doing if it does not deal with one of the great subjects of contemporary social concern, so a junior programme took as its theme over three visits the misuse of the Earth's resources.[71] In the first visit, a comic run-down of the whole history of the negligent, acquisitive white man in America was contrasted with the indigenous Indian's close, caring and balanced understanding of his environ-

Give us back our sea (*This Rare Earth*)

ment; the second session dealt with the struggle for compensation of the Japanese villagers stricken by mercury poisoning from chemical effluent; in the third, the children played a simulation game based on the United Nations. The classes of nine-year-olds whom I observed certainly enjoyed it, as it was presented with great skill; by the admission of one of the company, however, few of them were able to make the enormous transfer from one part to the next, in order to understand the common implications for human survival of this brave, but rather ambitious programme.

Themes of social moment and contemporary concern are an important proportion of the subject matter of TIE; perhaps more than in adult drama it is often more effective to present a microcosmic, a dramatic situation with elements small and individualised enough for the children to comprehend, empathise and therefore deeply identify with. Show them an epitome and give them the tools and motivation to explore the wider implications for themselves. For this reason, the threatened community of a village duckpond or a vacant site may be a more valid symbol for the greedy or wanton spoliation of the environment than the ecological history of a continent.

Teachers and actors

'Teaching is very close to acting for both the actor and the teacher are set apart from their audiences ... they both exist through their capacity to entertain or to capture the interest and enthusiasm of the audience they serve.... Actor and teacher must plan his performance and acquire his techniques of handling his audience and of putting his material over.... Both of them project and overstate at times ... and neither actor nor teacher are quite what they seem' (Gerald Tyler).[72]

So far, so very succinct a summary of the similarities; but it is not so easy as that. There are important differences too, as I have already implied, notably in the kind of experience they offer their audiences. Though they share many techniques and ranges of posture, each traditionally has a dimension which is not available to the other. For example, interaction is a vital element in a teaching situation—or, as it is now more often considered, a learning situation. Few teachers merely lecture to their passive students; there must always be an active response, though he can limit the quality and quantity of that response. On the simplest level, the response is necessary for the teacher to assess how much effect his teaching has had. Much more important, it is now becoming increasingly recognised in practice that the children's response is perhaps the most important part of the learning process itself, when the concepts are crystallised and tried out. With this realisation, the teacher more and more steps off the centre stage, and sets up contexts where the children control their own material and pace of learning, and he provides the initial and continuing stimulus—the prologue and prompter, if you like. Interaction in a 'pure' play is always extrinsic, whether helping to create a shared atmosphere or throwing tomatoes. The actors are in total control of their material, which cannot be altered by the respondents.

To say that 'neither actor nor teacher are quite what they seem' is a cunning half-truth, misleading in the use of that word 'quite'. An actor, in a part, is not at all what he seems: he is a character in a prescribed context outside which he is not responsible for what happens inside. This dissociation is true even if he is 'playing' a character which bears strong specific likenesses to his own personality, drawing from the personae in which he operates in real life. (It is even still true, though harder to differentiate, if the actor absorbs aspects of characterisation into those personae, behaving in a similarly type-cast fashion on and off stage.)

The actor takes absolute responsibility for his material on stage, but only there; the teacher shares the responsibility inside and outside the classroom. The actor/teacher using some measure of integrated active response from the children as part of the programme gives over some of the responsibility for the performance to the audience; he should (and most actor/teachers do) therefore acknowledge some responsibility towards the continuing learning process, by way of follow-up work, or preparation, or the attempt to provide an experience relevant to some aspect of the curriculum in its narrower or wider sense.

Essentially the complex mystiques and training rituals of the two trades boil down to these factors. Each is a job for which the most important requirements are (*a*) a clear understanding of one's role in relation to a group of recipients; (*b*) an equally clear recognition of their needs; (*c*) a grasp of the material sufficient to supply those needs; and (*d*) the experience to select an appropriate strategy in the use of the material to satisfy the needs.

Traditionally actor and teacher alike, concerned with 'The Drama' or 'My Subject' might put (*c*) and (*d*) before (*a*) and (*b*); an actor/teacher must not. As soon as he regards the material as important as an end in itself, rather than merely the means,

Teaching in role (*The Fire of London*)

he is entering dangerous didactic territory, and his programme ceases to be flexible, pupil-centred, or open-ended. To assist the development of these four qualities, training is usually demanded (always in teaching). But what kind of training? These days, Colleges of Education teach acting, and Drama Schools run teacher-training courses, both of which probably help to develop these related but disparate skills. In the end, however, sows' ears are immutable, and silk purses take time and practice to make. It is as hard for the trained teacher to avoid oozing teacherliness in the theatrical dimension as it is for the actor not to strut actorially in the interactive.

New moves

Recent developments suggest that the actor/teacher's responsibilities are expanding in at least three directions which can be loosely termed Downwards, Upwards, and Outwards.

Downwards At the moment there is a great deal of enthusiasm for theatre in education in Colleges of Education, but when the students leave, having done their hurried compulsory or voluntary programme, squeezed into the course and performed once or twice, very few outlets. The interest from inside that this is generating among drama teachers is manifesting itself in schools, where they are infecting the older students with their own enthusiasm. Designing a TIE programme for younger children, in junior schools or even in their own school, is becoming a not infrequent part of courageous C.S.E. Drama syllabuses, sixth-form Drama courses and Youth Theatre work. The standard is often surprisingly high, because the students are still close enough to childhood, and linked to it by younger brothers and sisters, to know clearly what the likes and needs are, so that although it often lacks sophistication and polish, naturally, it can find its target accurately—if the controlling teacher is good enough. As TIE becomes more widely known as a technique rather than a philosophy, this trend is going to increase among teachers who reject the ideas that educational drama with seniors should be merely a training in theatre skills, or a literary exercise in dramaturgy, but need clear objectives and specific goals on which to hang the improvisation that is the core of their work. In order for them to avoid all the dangers outlined throughout this volume, they need help and training from experts (that is, those who have already made a lot of mistakes, and learned from them). Some TIE teams are already aware of this responsibility and, as well as running courses for students, give elementary in-service training in TIE besides seminars and discussions on related aspects of drama teaching.

Upwards Simulations, casework and role-play are increasingly being used in training for adults: courses for managers, teachers, nurses, and others for whom recognising, avoiding and resolving problems of human relationships are important parts of their jobs, use these techniques to give the students the opportunity to practise strategies in a dynamic environment free from consequences. There are several opportunities for TIE here, too. Casework, though a useful teaching technique, tends to be rather abstract, proceeding as it does by verbal discussion which does not always highlight the more complex and less predictable interaction processes; role-play by itself, though it does highlight them better, is often selfconsciously artificial and can easily develop into over-simplified confrontations that teach nothing. The use of actor/teachers can produce a learning situation which may be tangibly tested, yet can be structured enough to focus the students' attentions on the essentials and the overall picture—help them see the wood and the trees. For instance, a group of middle-management executives need training in interviewing techniques; they are split into four groups, each endowed as a 'selection panel'. They are given the background of a job selection situation, and a rough guide to the kind of candidate they are looking for. Then, in turn, but in different order, each panel interviews all four 'candidates', actor/teachers who have assumed a personality with clearly defined strengths and weaknesses, carefully contrasted with each other. The four groups then make their order of preference, and pool their findings. When this was used on one adult course it proved of limited value in training insight into character, because obviously real characters are far more complex than the stereotypes of the actors' characterisations, their weaknesses better disguised, though the exercise did point out in a lively way some of the traits to look for. Its main value lay in isolating and crystallising in the students' minds the priorities that each individual *really* had, the differences in how each viewed the job, and the qualities that deep-down he thought most desirable and undesirable.[73]

Another technique found useful with adults is an extension of the role-questioning used in many secondary programmes; the actor/teachers enact a situation leading to a crisis, the students question them in role, then decide on a course of action—perhaps followed by the actor/teachers improvising possible consequences of that action if they are confident enough. A variant of this is to enact the scene, ask the students to identify and discuss the crucial errors in judgment or human relationships, then re-enact it, with the students stopping it at these points to advise the characters what they should do instead. This has been done in America, apparently with great success, on film—with the students stopping the film at the crucial points to discuss them with the tutor.[74] The great advantage of using live actors is that the students' solutions can be tried out in front of them, even *by* them if they are confident enough themselves to role-play.

Live actors are quite useful to have around in simulation exercises like board meetings, to keep in reserve, well-briefed, to be called upon when necessary as a mouthpiece, or to test out a decision. (What would X say? Who would need to be consulted first? Should we now bring in the leader of the deputation whose petition is being considered?)

This whole potentially fertile area for theatre in education is scarcely measured yet, much less ploughed; hopelessly over-worked as they are by the demands of the primary and secondary schools, TIE teams today cannot afford the luxury of cultivating the exalted field of tertiary education, which must probably lie fallow for a good while yet.

... and Outwards Right from its start TIE has been very socially conscious; within its basic common philosophy lies embedded the desire to perform a community service, mainly through the schools, mainly to the young; this is why the strength of the movement has always lain in the *local* groups—at the time of writing, virtually all the companies which claim TIE as the majority of their work operate within one education authority, in as small a locality as their financial backers will allow. Relationships with schools close enough to ensure useful context work, an understanding of the particular area, its problems, needs, history, ethos, and mythologies, and a sense of continuity, regularity and dependability are the advantages of a restricted working area. As teams become involved in exploring the preoccupations of their areas in their programmes, they inevitably move into fields of relevance beyond the schools, and start thinking outwards towards the community as a whole.

Encouragement for this comes from many directions. Community arts centres, usually financed by Regional Arts Associations, are springing up all over England; local plays about local themes, when well enough written and not patronising, have been expanding the social register of theatregoers in Stoke on Trent and Glasgow, Stratford East and Newcastle, along with box-office receipts; most important is the trend towards community politics. As popular participation in decision-making and decision-changing is seen to be desirable, perhaps attainable, and certainly fashionable, education in the issues on which the people have powers of action becomes essential, and theatre, as a direct method of communication and education, is harnessed. At their most trivial, teams can feed their ideologies on a local problem, whip up a sententious indignation, and descend on an area with a polemic whose concern, the audience usually quickly realises, is spurious; at their best, sensitive in their work all the time to the flow of life within *their* community, they can respond to the need by presenting burning issues clearly, challengingly and directly, responsible only to their audiences, but entirely to them, for the messages they bring and the solutions they suggest.

More and more teams are trying to find time to spend working in community centres, parks and playgrounds, pubs and clubs, two at least already with the specific backing of a nationally financed social experiment.[75]

Chapter Seven

Responsibilities

Looking after the customers

Some reservations of teachers and local authority drama advisers have already been extensively quoted. To restore the balance—in fact, most teachers are gratefully enthusiastic about most of the TIE opportunities they are offered, and most advisers are wholeheartedly appreciative of the good work being done, in patches, all over Britain, though experience has sometimes tempered this appreciation with caution. Their position makes some advisers very aware of the degree of responsibility with which a company approaches its work. It is easy to be irresponsible; when you are flitting from one school or borough to the next, offering a single experience, wrapped in glamour and with little comeback, a sense of responsibility must be self-imposed. And there are important responsibilities if the experience is not to be merely a trivial one. Most important are those to the children; I have already implied some of the dangers, to which there are no easy solutions, only questions which the teams must constantly face.

If young children are to be stirred, profoundly, they may have to experience degrees of fear or anxiety and 'live through the experience to the happy ending'. By choosing an incompetent but friendly witch as the Link in an infant programme,[51] one team neatly engineered a situation of logical fantasy in which the children became involved absolutely naturally. Most enjoyed this, and participated willingly and fully. To a few, a *witch* had connotations too strong to overcome, and when they were presented with other fearful stimuli—an angry king, and, more important, his bodyguard with a big, real sword—these children had nobody they dared to turn to for security, and spent the rest of what had been for them an unhappy morning on their teacher's lap. These may have been exceptionally nervous children, but how justifiable is it to sacrifice the quietude of the 'special cases' to provide the majority with an experience which is not gutless? In small-audience participation work it is often possible and advisable to discuss the programme in advance, and identify the potential 'problem' children for whom special dispensation can be made within the programme. Children, though, do not always act predictably, and the teachers do not know everything about their pupils.

·This problem and another were highlighted in an experimental programme for much older children.[15] A 'social worker', giving a talk to fifteen-year-olds about his casework, described an example of a particularly difficult case, where a boy had just been taken into care. The 'worker' went out on a pretext, and a moment later 'this boy's father' stormed in, dirty, inarticulate, over six feet tall and very aggressive, demanding to see the 'social worker'. In the next twenty minutes the students were first of all left alone with him, then they watched a confrontation where the 'father' put his case; after this they discussed it with the 'social worker' and eventually tried to explain their decisions to the 'father'. Only towards the end did they realise that the situation was a drama; there was nothing in the format to show them it was not real. In the first performance the 'father' underestimated the theatricality of his entrance, and by overplaying it he caused genuine panic where the students sat really paralysed with fright and suffered for five minutes alone with what they thought was a dangerous lunatic. How far was that justifiable? The students, afterwards, were divided; the actor thought it was not, and drastically changed the characterisation for the next performance, to lessen the fear, and create a measure of pity or amusement. Subsequent performances were unanimously approved by the students, and achieved much readier interaction, but there is no doubt that the experience, if pleasanter, was much less memorable and pungent.

More important, perhaps, was it justifiable to deceive the audience into believing, even temporarily, a spurious reality—a trick often used in secondary school TIE programmes? An experienced observer eminent in the field of educational drama commented tartly:

'We spend so much time talking about the strength of "the dramatic experience" and children's ability to suspend their disbelief, and then we don't trust them to identify, preferring to "con" them instead.'

There was a measure of disagreement within the team about one notable programme, which purported to be a 'town planning course' run by 'The Council for Environmental

No clue it is a theatre (*Holland New Town*)

Education',[76] and including group work sessions taken by people involved in a supposed New Town being built nearby. As these sessions developed, very subtly and ingeniously, hints of corruption emerged, involving three of the protagonists. The other two led the students into an investigation of this corruption, during which they learned a lot about the priorities and expediencies involved in community planning, as well as gaining insight into how the possibility of corruption can arise, and even sometimes be very difficult to avoid. The 'reality'—utterly convincing to most of the pupils, though one or two had their doubts—gave an atmosphere of tense excitement that steadily grew from the necessarily very slow start till the sense of conspiracy and 'real-life' adventure was nerve-racking, and provided ample justification for this framework of subterfuge. On the other hand, it has its disadvantages, which two of the team thought crucial: to establish verisimilitude, the plot had to be unfolded very slowly, so that by the end of the first session, in the performance I saw, two disaffected students who were bored by town planning and did not realise that there was more excitement in store than just that, decided not to return. The simulation group sessions were of rather peripheral import-ance to the real plot, and lacked deep commitment to their real, if indirect, relevance; perhaps, if the students had known they were taking part in simulation, and why, they might have invoked their conscious wills to better purpose. Most of all, when at the end the team very properly dropped all pretence, the response and discussion showed genuine interest, but about the feeling of realisation that it was a play, not about the implications of corruption in town planning. Whichever way the programme had been played, something would have been both gained and lost.

Though young people are quick to spot and resent exploitation, the students, both in this programme and the other about the social worker, accepted the convention, saying more or less unanimously that they preferred not being told that it was 'only a play'—the surprise elements were more powerfully thought-provoking; even the first class who suffered the fright of the angry father, while they felt it had been overdone, approved the technique. An interesting individual reaction to this programme which underlines another questionable aspect was that of a boy, normally an isolate, who was the first person to dare to speak to 'the father', while nobody was sure whether it was real or drama; this action enormously enhanced his esteem in the eyes of the rest, who appreciated his real courage and complimented him warmly afterwards. *That* manifestation was unquestionably a good side-effect of the programme, but suppose somebody under the spell of the 'reality' had reacted in a way that would reduce his esteem, by bursting into tears, or running out of the room? The protective irresponsibility is withheld from the children; the actors are only acting, but the audience is reacting in real life.

There are of course no easy answers to these rhetorical questions; the shock of plunging the audience unexpectedly into a theatrical adventure can be one of the most devastatingly effective techniques a team can use to create involvement. The answers lie in each team's hands, to judge for themselves, from their knowledge of each audience, where the line between stimulation and exploitation falls, though perhaps one factor to help them is the degree of pure pleasure the programme affords; if a programme is fun, does it matter if the children never know they have been tricked? If, on the other hand, pity, fear, concern, revulsion, anxiety, or other strong, serious emotions are being aroused, it must surely be unethical under any circumstances not to allow the children to assert their disbelief, to reject what the team has to offer if the model cannot be made to fit their perception of the truth: that is replacing drama with deceit.

Both the town planning and the social worker programmes were painstakingly open-ended, with social work and planning procedures scrupulously researched, and value judgments avoided, as well as glib moralising. It might not have been so. In a medium of communication and education where heroes and villains are the order of the day, it is hard not to let biases and prejudices show. Dramatic cases can conceal generalised attitudes. Whatever one's personal beliefs, how justifiable was it, in a junior school programme about an ecological disaster caused by irresponsible nuclear testing at the North Pole,[59] to present the French Government, embodied in the villain of the piece, as the sole agent of irresponsible and cowardly deceitfulness, without really getting a fair chance to express his position? Remember, the disaster, though conceivable, was fictitious. The slanting of opinion into fact is just as dangerous when it is implicit or unconscious. A programme mentioned earlier[27] implied a cause for schizophrenia that might be described as 'layman's Laing', and tacitly suggested, by not mentioning any alternative dimensions or explanatory factors, that this was simply and incontrovertibly the cause of the illness.

The potholes are just as deep to the right of centre, where programmes, and the mental health of the audience, are threatened by the disease of moralysis, known chiefly through its main symptom: an increasingly sclerotic sanctimoniousness. English policemen, for instance, are no more the eternally kind and upright pillars of a just society than they are the bent and vicious instruments of a brutal decadence; either picture panders to the preconceptions of some of the audience, and pandering is no business of theatre in education.

Does this mean that programmes must everlastingly present a bland objectivity, no viewpoint presented without being immediately cancelled by its opposite? To suggest this would be unrealistic as well as unnecessary, since most of the people, amateur or professional, who wish to spend their time preparing and presenting TIE programmes for youngsters are very committed to the work; they have ideas and opinions which they want to communicate forcefully because they believe in them deeply. Art that never takes sides is usually insipid, and deep conviction is one of the mainsprings of both dramatic tension and poetic feeling.

The dangers of preaching, whether subservience or sedition, are quite easily avoided in practice, by a seasoning of critical humour and the open-door principle. Statements of social, political or spiritual belief, no matter how passionate or controversial, are valid, in fact absolutely essential in an educational situation, provided the children have an exit clearly marked, that the programme recognises the possibility of fallibility. The more the material points one way, the more clearly signposted must be the exit. Young people appreciate an honest offer and respond to enthusiastic sincerity, but are unlikely anyway to believe a programme that pretends to a hot line to the Fount. It is true that the 'static' forces of most of their education and environmental conditioning have provided them with the certainties demanded by young childhood and continued long after, and some adolescents happily accept these, rejecting any fleeting impressions that might rock their security; others are starting to question and reject them, so sense with distrust efforts from 'the other side' to bypass their critical examination with more certainties. A programme that uses the depth and intensity of passionate conviction to probe and question, opening up new avenues and inviting the students to explore them, is likely to be better received by the students themselves, as well as by their more discerning teachers, than one which merely provides shrill answers.

The most direct responsibility that actor/teachers have to their audiences is to be aware throughout the programme of its impact on them, to monitor their responses with far more sensitivity than actors on an adult stage need, so that they can temper their own performances appropriately to create the strongest desirable effect. They need to be able to respond to the first hint of restlessness or incipient over-reaction, or distinguish between fear that is enjoyable and sheer terror. Most important of all, they must stay sufficiently detached to respond with conscious consideration, not instinctively, because instinctive responses tend to relate to the actor/teacher's security rather than the children's need. For example, a common blunder occurs if the children are fidgeting or over-reacting because they are confused, or because peripheral participation has been invoked without clear boundaries; if for some reason the programme is not striking home clearly, we often instinctively assume that the theatricality is not vivid enough, and, fighting to regain ascendancy, we redouble our efforts to impress the audience and go over the top. As often as not this redoubles our problems, because the children's minds are not under-employed but overwhelmed, bemused by the strength of images they cannot fit together. At this point, if we are teachers watching, we usually react wrongly, too; our sympathy leaps towards the struggling actors and we have difficulty restraining ourselves from a demonstration of 'discipline' to restore security to the theatrical arena, at the very least by a whispered rebuke to those within range followed usually by a little homily after the show about the bad behaviour and impoliteness to the actors who were so kindly giving us all such a treat. Emphatically, this is wrong; the actors (who are usually getting paid anyway for their 'kindness') have among their own equipment of skills the means of restoring interest and attention to the programme. If they have not today, they soon will have. The teacher will normally accomplish nothing by intervening, except to establish the concept that he is in league with the silly people on stage, therefore just as silly as they are. Only *in extremis*, if one or two irreclaimables are spoiling the sincere enjoyment of the many, or if the hall is about to be wrecked, is it justifiable to step in.

The teacher's function

This does not mean that the teacher is without a role, better off out of the way while the actors get on with the show uninterrupted. For one thing, the vital concept of the TIE programme as being the central focus of an ongoing process comprising preparation, performance and follow-up, essentially linked to the child's schooling, would be impossible without the incorporation and co-operation of the class teacher. Even during the performance itself, the presence of the teacher as an unobtrusive participant is doubly important. First, he is taking part in a shared experience with his children, who invariably appreciate this—they like to be able to check their own impressions with somebody whose understanding they acknowledge to be greater than theirs, and it can even briefly create an almost conspiratorial atmosphere between him and them. Second, and especially with young children, the teacher can be on hand if anything goes wrong—an actor cannot at any time and without difficulty detach himself to deal with a child who is suddenly unwell, or wets himself with excitement; sometimes even a well-devised Link character is not security enough for a frightened child, who needs a *familiar* lap. This is usually, but not always, recognised by schools, so that one company was forced to plead in its booking prospectus, with polite acidity:

> 'When we visit a school it is expected that the same teacher who has been involved in the preparatory work will be present in a passive role during the visit. If there is absenteeism among the staff, whilst sympathising with the school's problem, we are not supply teachers and cannot be used as such, which means that we are not able to take all or part of another class that is without a teacher, and that the teacher who is due to be with us should not be asked to take another class instead of observing the programme.'[77]

Teacher-participation was particularly important for this company, who have a highly developed approach to follow-up work, based on their use of preparatory workshops. There is a little controversy over the advisability of preparing follow-up work for teachers; some teams feel that the theatrical experience should stand alone, and not be watered down by bathetic school-work; others, with undue and untypical humility, maintain that it would be presumptuous of them to tell teachers what to do. Actor/teachers must face that, whether they like it or not, some teachers are going to use their programme in some way or other—it is too valuable a stimulus not to. On the other hand, since all teachers are not necessarily imaginative or inventive, some will waste the opportunities the programme offers by doing nothing, and others will pervert its purpose by mis-understanding it, or misusing it to do work which takes all the joy out of it for the children; all these need help, and most welcome it.

Abuse can be almost obviated, and other functions served, by the team holding a preliminary workshop to which all the teachers whose classes are to receive the pro-gramme are invited. These workshops usually take the form of the actor/teachers either explaining or experimentally acting out their programme, followed by a two-way discussion. Several major companies use this device, which seems to me entirely admirable. As an absolute priority, they can help the teachers to understand the exact point of the programme, and exactly what is required. Use of a workshop would have prevented the misunderstanding which spoilt one performance of *The Ballad of Billy Martin*, and countless others to which inappropriate children are invited, where the teacher, with misplaced kindness and disregarding the preliminary handout, arranged for some eleven-year-olds to watch a performance of this programme which was well beyond them, and with which they could not cope emotionally or intellectually. In workshops, aspects of work surrounding the programme can be explored; the actors may have prepared a sequence of introductory tasks to be done before the performance itself, for which the teachers can be prepared. Suggestions for interim or follow-up work can be discussed, and a two-way element introduced as the team and the teachers together explore possible avenues and design the contextual work as a combined effort. The various dangers can be pointed out, such as providing sterile, dreary tasks that vitiate the performance. Teachers are not always better than actor/teachers at stimulating positive discussion, and may need help to point out the possibilities; in some cases, discussion may be necessary to emphasise the programme's point, in others, to resolve and rationalise residues of direct fear or grief into understanding concern. In others still, no discussion at all may be the order of the day, and this teachers need to be told; the children may want to think, paint, build, act out, write or talk amongst themselves about their response to the programme; a 'discussion' in the style of 'right and wrong answers' with the teacher, which just goes over points that have already registered, is often worthless and demeaning. A workshop is also a good place to test out the acceptability of the programme's ideas. Written résumés are often misleading, and after a programme is too late for teachers' reservations to have any effect. Controversial material or techniques can be discussed, and the team given a favourable environment to justify them; teachers may even be asked to suggest modifications to the programme as it stands, which would give the team a bank of alternatives to try out in practice.

Even workshops are not infallible against rampant ignorance, however: part of one programme,[71] preceded by a thorough workshop and a very full written synopsis, clearly had as its theme how Red Indians instinctively respected their environment, and formed their life style to live in ecological peace; clearly enough for all the children, but not the teacher, who spent twenty minutes of laboured questions warping their understanding of the theme into romanticised nonsense summed up as 'You see, the Indians never fought among themselves; they all had relatives in the other tribes and helped each other.' (Verbatim!)

'Follow-up' work is the rather inaccurate general term used to cover the various types of context work that can surround a well-prepared programme. Preliminary work can serve several distinct functions. The children can be given in advance background on the general area of the subject matter, that will help them to understand the programme better, which in turn will illuminate their understanding of the whole subject. Without realising it, the children may be working for an eventual unexpected and specific satisfaction that occurs during the performance itself; having helped a king solve his problems, the children were ecstatic when he asked them if they would show him some of their recent work, which 'happened' to be about palaces and kings. The preliminary work may be in order to prepare materials for use in the programme itself; for one about a village fair,[78] the children had previously practised 'tricks and games and shows' in drama lessons, as well as each making a coloured paper leaf to stick on Tom Tiddler's magic tree. This kind of preliminary work is usually best done by the class teacher, for reasons of economy as much as the desire to retain the full impact of surprise and theatricality. There are exceptions, like *Ghost in the Village*, where the opening piece of theatre by the actor/teachers, sketching in the background, provided the springboard for the interim work by the class teacher with the 'archive pack'.

To overcome the problem of 'drama-readiness' in areas with few drama-trained teachers, some actor/teachers visit the schools in advance, as peripatetic drama specialists, giving an educational drama lesson as warming-up practice, for children who are to take part in programmes with a high degree of integral participation.

There is a danger of follow-up work after a programme petering out gradually in a dreary anti-climax, so it is probably wise for teams, rather than just giving vague suggestions for teachers to follow if they choose, to prepare a fairly self-contained sequence, structured to contain the implications they hope will be explored, and suggesting an appropriate ending to the project. Some teachers will gratefully cling to it, delighted to have the preparation taken off their hands, but there is nothing to stop the confident or imaginative just using it at his discretion, or as a jumping-off point; by preparing it, the team have made their own intentions and expectations clear.

The team which devised *Tom Tiddler's Ground* encouraged follow-up work with a bombardment of useful material—articles from newspapers, pictures, photographs, maps, games, quizzes, statistics, collages—at first daunting, but so stimulatingly chosen and presented that it would take a very dull-witted teacher not to respond to it enthusiastically and make something of it.

Over-all responsibilities: the team and the system

Ideally, if the team is carrying out its responsibility to the pupils, then it must also be fulfilling its duty towards their parents and teachers. In practice it is not so easy, since most heads, many teachers and quite a few parents know with certainty that their own attitudes and the place they occupy on the educational continuum are exactly right for *their* children, and so tend to see any approach from another point on it as either debilitating or corrupting; one teacher's charming tale is another's feeble fable, one's potent stimulus another's dangerous meddling. Some companies have found it tempting, in a position insecure in terms of finance and status, to play safe and give the teachers what the team imagines the teachers expect, keeping all their material in safe proximity to the curriculum, or so uncontroversial that the most aggressively conservative teacher or parent could only say, 'How nice!' I believe that this is failing to carry out one's responsibility to the children, or to those 'more discerning teachers'. It is no more necessary to pander to the lowest expectations of teachers and parents than those of children. Having first of all established its own philosophy and criteria, a responsible company presents programmes which stretch the audience and present a new angle for the teacher. Intelligence, skill and conviction are very persuasive, and the great majority of teachers and parents are open, or at least vulnerable, to them. The weakness of theatre in education, that it is a minuscule proportion of the schooling experience, can be its strength in this context; it can without too much risk for them, open new doors for the teachers who have perhaps neither time, co-operation nor backing to dare to experiment on people committed to their care for long periods. The teachers themselves have the opportunity to sit back and observe a condensed educational experiment in action, then take it over in the follow-up work. At certain points the boundary is very narrow between helping teachers by pushing them further forward than they would dare, and outraging them so much that they throw the team out.

TIE companies can also slip into the easy delusion that on their shoulders alone rests the mantle of progressive education, and 'regular' teachers are all forces for repression or passivity. On a sunny day I heard two actor/teachers agreeing self-righteously that, 'They should all be let out on a day like this, not kept cooped up in there', as they passed a school window from which a local folk-song was emanating (a piece of sub-Thoreau reasoning which quite forgot that their own programme that afternoon would take place in a darkened studio!).

For most of the time these dangers can be easily avoided by conscientious liaison between teams and teachers. Where this exists, teams sometimes chafe at their loss of autonomy, and it is certainly true that they have occasionally had their wings cruelly and unjustifiably clipped by a dull and over-cautious liaison panel, or drama adviser. On the other hand, it is no bad thing to be forced to justify controversial material to test its acceptability; if the critical criteria are sufficiently agreed on (admittedly, on occasion they are not), it is a useful discipline. If it cannot be justified convincingly, should it be performed? After all, teachers do know children. Usually, all that is needed is trust, a close and understanding relationship based on the team's reputation for maturity, reliability, openness to ideas from within the system, and above all, the quality of their product, so that teachers are content to leave matters in their hands, knowing that decisions made by the team will be backed up by intelligent and responsible commitment. This kind of relationship has been built up by the best of the locally based groups, who can put in their programmes notes like this, confident that they will not be misunderstood or attacked:

> 'The material now being prepared [a documentary play for sixth formers about the status of women in our society] is consciously revolutionary and deliberately designed to provoke strong feelings in the discussions we hope you will hold in your classroom after the performance. In dealing with such a subject there will inevitably be mention of sexual relationships between men and women, and of contraception. However you can feel confident that the production does not set out deliberately to embarrass the audience.'[70]

It is often details, rather than over-all intent, that irritate teachers—details like a thoughtless disregard for the problems of the institution, by companies who arrive late with badly-made scenery that gouges the hall floor, barely condescend to talk to the teachers, and leave the hall in chaos after them. Another provocation is the team who decide that the quickest way to the approval of the pupils and the boosting of their own egos is to set themselves up as the children's champions in defying the system, and portray among their characters stupid, bullying teachers, nagging, stubborn parents and similar caricatures, hoping that by implication the students will see the team's self-identifying hero as their rebel champion and rescuer. Teachers ought not to treat this kind of characterisation too anxiously or humourlessly; whatever the team's motivation or level of maturity, the transient and literally inconsequential nature of the theatrical experience means that at the worst the children are provided with a harmless safety valve if they want it. Besides, a well-directed prick to teachers' own egos from a team that knows what it is doing, and doing it deliberately but not maliciously, is a salutary antidote to their sense of their own importance.

The charlatans are the exceptions; most practitioners of theatre in education, groping in this new field, and with widely differing amounts of talent and experience, are enthusiastically doing their best to cater for a need that is only just being recognised; they deserve the help and trust that allows them freedom to experiment, make mistakes and disappear up blind alleys; only by risking failure can the boundaries of success be mapped, and the value be understood.

Theatre in education that is self-regarding or destructive is neither more nor less than trivial. It only becomes significant when, recognising the extreme limitations of its own position, it sets out with clear objectives to make a positive contribution to the process of education in its widest sense. Then it becomes a valuable source of excitement, of stimuli and of challenge, that should be permanently available to every child, not just to the few in the couple of dozen or so boroughs who so far (1975) believe a permanent company is worth paying for.

The real effect of participation—an experiment

In a recent article,[79] the authors described some experimental work in theatre for young children using different kinds of involvement; three plays were designed and performed, one keeping the children as spectators, one allowing partial participation, and the third invoking 'full' participation. As the writers had expected:

'The most total recall of actual events was in the first play, and although the children had been most physically involved with the third, their memory of the total picture was confused and partial.'

Though the authors felt that, 'There was a greater immediate depth of imaginative involvement by the children participating in the latter,' their conclusions were that:

'From his role as spectator the child gains a deeper understanding of the story, of the over-all conflict and of the moral questions the play poses as an entirety.... Our aims should be limited and ... part of that limitation is that we don't try to both "tell a story" and, at the same time, create a remembered event of value in which the child participates.'

The findings of this article, which were asserted very definitely, appeared to run entirely counter to what seemed to have been my experience, as epitomised in the last paragraph of Chapter 5. It is easy to be carried away by self-indulgent enthusiasm, so this might be a very useful piece of deflation and disillusioning. On the other hand, as the experiment was not described in detail, it was impossible to know how integral, how strongly established—or how successful—the participation had been, or to what extent the experiment had been carried out. Perhaps most importantly, the account did not say how much of a group experience the participation was. I have since discovered that in fact the children were very much involved as individuals, each immersed for much of the time in his own corner of a complex and intriguing plot, so it is not surprising that the 'memory of the total picture was confused and partial'. While realising that this in no way implies a value judgment, and that this very factor may well have enhanced the 'immediate depth of imaginative involvement', I was interested to discover if the same fragmented confusion would apply where the involvement had been a strong *group* experience. In addition, I was keen to challenge a colleague with a dislike of visual media of storytelling—particularly television, but also children's films and theatre—who maintained that a well-told story had the greatest impact, and that visual stimuli stood in the way of the child's comprehension by distracting him. Accordingly, to shed more light on the whole subject, and widen the scope of the original experiment, I devised an experiment of my own, with ten pairs of classes, in a preliminary attempt to discover the *real* effect of TIE where the participation is integral, total and shared as a group experience. Initially this was to try to discover the comparative depth and quality of recall, though it was expanded to measure other factors. I offer it not as definitive, but as useful, evidence which, as I am quoting it warts and all, may be profitably disputed.

Theatre in Education experiment 1974

General aims

Theoretical To attempt to throw light on:
(*a*) whether material taught in different ways is differently understood;
(*b*) to what extent, if any, total group participation affects understanding of dramatic story.

Practical In a preliminary way:
(*a*) to see if there are any differences in response to a TIE programme which is based on surprise and unpredictability, a told story, and a programme where the children are acting out a familiar story;
(*b*) to attempt to isolate factors in theatre in education with young children which are successful, and some of the problems.

Strategy

To present a TIE programme to ten classes of seven-year-old children, and have the same material, written as a story with all elements of possible theatre removed, read by the class teacher, to an equal number of parallel classes from the same schools. Both sets of classes would be asked to do the same simple visual and verbal follow-up work; after a week, the programme would be performed to those classes who had previously had it read to them. The two sets of follow-up work would be compared as objectively as possible.

Aims of Programme/Story

It must have a clear story-line, evolving naturally and smoothly, each element from the last, and a strong basic dramatic situation which could be understood clearly by seven-year-olds; this situation should involve:

(*a*)   a character with whose predicament the children could identify;

(*b*)   a character who could provide them with an emotional security from which, in the performance version, they could participate wholeheartedly;

(*c*)   a bad or naughty character to cause the dramatic conflict;

(*d*)   total physical and mental involvement of the children throughout, including both problem solving and decisive planning, as a group rather than individuals;

(*e*)   a happy ending;

(*f*)   the unusual glamour of a theatrical event;

(*g*)   a logical pattern not depending on fantasy;

(*h*)   elements of genuine surprise.

Because of the limitation imposed by the fact that there was only one actor/teacher (myself) to provide the experience—otherwise desirable, to cut down the performance variables—characters (*a*) and (*b*) had to be rolled into one, while (*c*) had to be represented by an invisible agent, recognised by the result of his actions and tape-recorded sound effects worked by the class teacher. This in turn meant that (*g*) could not be fully implemented.

Outline of the programme as performed

Earlier on the day of the programme the children receive a large coloured envelope addressed to them, containing the mysterious message:

'If you want to find YOU KNOW WHAT you will have to make and take the space machine to The Hall of Pretend and put the message together. Signed: P.'

The teacher, previously briefed, is as mystified as the children, and eventually the letter is put to one side, temporarily forgotten and unexplained.

Separately from this, the teacher will have announced the day before that the children are going to have a visit from the Songman, who is going to sing some songs with them. At the prescribed time the children go to the hall to meet the Songman, Fred, who introduces himself, establishing that he is friendly. He tells the children that sadly he cannot sing to them after all, because he has lost his guitar. Has any of them stolen it or seen it? When he finds out they have not, he tells them that it must have been The Pest. At this moment there is a screech of fiendish laughter coming from nowhere. 'There,' he tells the children, 'that's The Pest; we'd better whisper so that he can't hear us.' The Songman gathers the children round and tells them about The Pest, which is a mischievous, disembodied creature, that plays practical jokes, but usually leaves some sort of clue to his games. Has anything happened which could be a clue? The letter is remembered and discussed.

The Songman helps the children to build a space machine, either through occupational mime or with the use of apparatus in the hall; everybody climbs aboard and, aided by sound effects, travels to The Hall of Pretend. There they look for and find a number of cards, previously concealed, on each of which is written a word and a number. The children sort them out into numerical order, only to find that the message reads:

'Ha ha pest signed staffroom the or cloakrooms the of one or cupboard teacher's your in either is guitar the.'

The message is eventually reversed and understood; everybody climbs back into the space machine and travels back. Groups of children are dispatched to search the appropriate places, the guitar is found and brought back.

When the Songman tries to start his song at last, The Pest's laughter keeps interrupting to make the singing impossible, so the children have to work out a plan to outwit The Pest—helped by what they know of it already. Eventually one of their plans succeeds, The Pest is made to promise to be no more trouble, and there is just time for a song all together. When it is finished, Fred says:

'That's the end of the song; it's the end of The Pest too; and that means it's the end of the story, because it's all been only a story. Goodbye, children.' And he walks out.

The story as told

The story of this programme was re-written for the teachers to tell to the control classes, and started:

'Not very far away there is a school, just like yours; in it is a classroom, just like yours; in the classroom are some children, just like you. One day, when they went into their classroom they were surprised to find a big pink envelope addressed to them lying on the table...'

Virtually all direct speech had been cut out, and the teachers were asked to read the story exactly as written, though trying to make it as interesting as possible. At the point where The Pest was interrupting the singing, the story reads: '... whispering together, the children and Fred made a plan.' Here the teachers were instructed to stop the reading and discuss with the children what plan they would have made up if they had been the children in the story. Finally the teachers concluded the story with the children's plan, finishing: 'There's just time for a song before dinner, said the Songman.'

Variables

This was intended to be a preliminary and fairly informal study; it is not scientifically valid for the following reasons:

1 The number of children over-all was small statistically (10 + 10 classes: 239 + 240).
2 The schools were not all directly comparable:
   (*a*)   seven were first year juniors, three were top infants;
   (*b*)   in one school the 'programme' class were classified as B stream of ability, the 'control' class as A stream;
   (*c*)   in one of the infants' schools the programme class was on average six months younger than the control class;
   (*d*)   in one school, while the control class was a 'normal' first year junior class, the

other consisted of some first year children, with some backward second and third year children;

(*e*)   class sizes varied between 18 and 37;

(*f*)   performance conditions varied greatly, with hall size, the availability of apparatus, the expectations or inhibitions of the children regarding the use of the hall, the apparent 'drama-readiness' of the children, the obtrusiveness or concealment of the tape recorder and the degree of rapport established between the actor/teacher and the teacher working the tape recorder: all these factors seemed to affect the kind and the quality of the performance.

3 The control classes depended on the class teachers reading a story, and the amount of enthusiasm and skill of these teachers was an even more variable factor than had been envisaged.

4 The inconsistent degree of sensitivity of the actor/teacher to the children, as well as their varied moods and drama experience, also affected the programme.

(*Note:* Since the actor/teacher's performances were obviously all *more* consistent with each other than those of the teachers, one would have expected much more fluctuation of results if these two variables had been crucial.)

5 The story was originally conceived as a theatre in education programme, not as a story *per se*, and might not be ideal as a story to read (cutting out the theatrical elements which characterise most children's stories, the direct speech, characterisation, and opportunities for role-play by the reader all make it untypical and cast doubt on the validity of the programme/story comparison). I was, however, surprised at how interested the children were in the story, according to the teachers—it must have had the elements to keep the attention and enthusiasm of nearly all the control classes.

6 The assessment of the follow-up work was affected by other variables—see 'Analysis and conclusions', pages 152–7.

This very diversity, though expressed here rather negatively, and leading to statistical imprecision, proved at least as useful as hoped in preliminary highlighting of the factors which affect performances and responses. In spite of them, there seems to be a measure of consistency in the results.

Follow-up work

The children were asked to do two main tasks:

1 Write down as much of the story as they could remember.
2 Draw a picture of the children with their space machine.

Among the variables in the follow-up were:

(*a*)   it was undertaken sometimes immediately (especially in control classes), sometimes with a short break, and sometimes the following day;

(*b*)   it was undertaken with varying degrees of enthusiasm and sustainment (average length in words varied between classes from 17–70 in the infant schools, and from 34–295 in the juniors) which appeared to reflect both social background of the area and the children's expectations in writing and drawing;

(*c*)   sometimes the drawing was done before the writing, sometimes the reverse, and this seemed to have had a decisive effect;

(*d*)   in most classes there were one or two children who did only one piece of work; and

(*e*)   in one programme class, eleven of the children appeared to have done no writing, which affects the figures slightly.

Analysis and conclusions

Analysis The children's follow-up work was analysed according to the number of story elements clearly present in the re-telling. (The programme content had been broken down into its most important elements, eight in all, which were common to all performances.) A slight variable here: an element might be missed, or misinterpreted, if the child had difficulty with written expression.

In addition the over-all understanding was assessed according to whether it was:

(*a*)   over-all accurate (that is, there was a basic understanding of the development of the story from beginning to end, though not necessarily including all the elements);

(*b*)   unfinished (that is, for some reason the story was left in the middle, in conflict, without the finding of the guitar, tricking The Pest, and the final successful song);

(*c*)   confused (that is, if the elements were unclearly understood, bore no relationship to each other, or their order was so muddled that the child had no clear grasp of the story as a whole).

Here obviously the above variable operates even more strongly, along with the assessor's own subjectivity; it was frequently necessary to make a relative judgment, particularly on the issue of confusion, whether or not the elements mentioned were sufficiently muddled to justify a 'confused' classification.

In spite of all these variables, I think the results, perhaps surprisingly, are consistent and notable enough to be worth printing.

TABLE A

Percentage of summaries over-all accurate, confused, unfinished

School	Programme Classes			Control Classes		
	Accurate	Unfinished	Confused	Accurate	Unfinished	Confused
Deneside Infants[1]	50·0	25·0	25·0	33·3	46·7	20·0
Colegate Infants	75·0	15·0	10·0	26·3	15·8	57·9
Parkside Infants	52·4	19·0	28·6	8·7	87·0	4·3
Toner Avenue Juniors	35·7	50·0	24·3	12·0	80·0	8·0
East Boldon Juniors	75·0	13·9	11·1	56·7	18·9	24·4
Cestria Juniors	84·6	Nil	15·4	72·2	5·6	22·2
Southwick Juniors[2]	66·6	13·3	20·1	35·3	38·1	26·6
Houghton Juniors	74·2	3·2	22·6	58·3	25·0	16·7
Parkview Juniors[3]	68·4	5·3	26·5	15·4	65·4	19·2
St John's Juniors	68·2	13·6	18·2	15·6	73·7	10·5
Averages						
Infants Schools	59·1	19·7	21·2	22·9	49·7	27·4
Junior Schools	67·5	14·1	19·4	37·6	43·9	18·5
All Schools	65·0	14·8	20·2	33·4	45·6	21·0

[1] Programme class 6 months younger than control.
[2] Programme class B stream, control class A stream.
[3] Programme class included some older backward children.

TABLE B

1 Main elements of story included in summaries (in terms of number of children).
2 Approximate average length (in words).

Total number of children taking part in the experiment: Programme Classes = 239
Control Classes   = 240

479

Element	Programme Class	Control Class
The letter from the Pest	75	168
The Songman	220	189
The Pest	199	155
Finding the guitar	183	173
Building and travelling in the Space Machine	160	130
Finding and decoding the clues	113	71
Planning to foil the Pest	81	42
Happy resolution	129	56
Average number of elements included per summary	4·73	3·97
Approximate average length (in number of words)		
Infants Schools	50	40
Junior Schools	90	122
All Schools	82	102

Tentative conclusions Obviously, in the light of all the variables, it would be wise not to place too much reliance on the statistics, but one or two points seem to be very clearly emphasised. The results have an interesting consistency, which suggests that none of these variables was crucial.

1 The programme classes appear to show a much better over-all grasp of the story (the figures back up my very strong subjective impressions) and they are better able to follow the story through to the finish. I do not think this was just better motivation to write, though this may have been a factor. Every single school, including the three where the odds might be said to be weighted against them, showed a markedly higher proportion of accurate summaries from the programme classes.

2 The programme classes appeared to have a better grasp of the important elements of the story. This is shown slightly in the average figures, perhaps unbalanced by the 'letter'; this was the only element of the eight which was mentioned by more of the control class children—not surprisingly, as it is the first thing mentioned in the story, and strongly emphasised, whereas, in the programme, though it makes a big impact, it is almost a thing apart from the main storyline.

3 Perhaps unexpectedly, there was little difference in length, with the control classes usually writing fractionally more. Taken in conjunction with point 1, my impression is that the programme classes were able to write much more succinctly, able to express the story simply and clearly; the control classes were longer, more imprecise and repetitive—the older the children, the truer this seemed.

The Pictures There were three variables here, too:

(a) Whether the pictures were drawn before or after the writing.

(b) The materials used, which varied from lead pencils to wax blocks, and from cartridge paper 30″/20″ to newsprint 9″/7″.

(c) The kind of art teaching used in the class, the emphasis put on art by the class teacher, and the techniques he taught.

However, again one or two general points seem to emerge.

Predictably, the programme classes drew what they saw; where they had built a space machine from imagination they usually included details of the hall; where it was made from the apparatus they usually drew it very accurately. The control classes always drew schematic stereotypes. One programme class was an exception to this, with, interestingly, eleven schematic machines; one control class took the opportunity to invent ingenious contraptions.

Very noticeable was the much fuller use of space by the programme classes; in all classes the paper was filled over-all by most of the children; control class drawings tended to be more fragmented. The subjective impression of a well-qualified observer, who did not know which were which, was that the programme class work showed on the whole much more 'spontaneity, exhilaration and enjoyment'. In their work, the detail was usually relevant; where there was detail in control class drawings, it was often purely decorative and unrelated to the story. Usually, though by no means in every case, there were more people in programme class drawings, and the people more individualised. There was more movement, while control class work tended to be rather static. Programme class work seemed to reflect a strong *class* experience—each class seemed coherent, the drawings recognisably of a piece.

Performances The performances with the control classes, who already knew the story, certainly had a different atmosphere about them, though to a smaller degree than I had expected. They were slightly less deeply involved, on the whole, though all enjoyed the programme, and all except one class were very co-operative and easily manageable, very enthusiastic. They sometimes became quite cross if we departed from the story as they remembered it—which often happened, if for example the plan which they had worked out in discussion was rather feeble, when I would arrange for it not to work in order to make them stretch their imaginations a little harder. Performances showed the importance, with young children, of a slow, gentle approach, the theatricality present, but muted; too much 'attack' merely confuses, frightens, or over-excites them; especially at the beginning they needed time to adjust to the conventions and characters —hence, in most infant work, the importance of the 'Link'.

I was surprised that the belief seemed much deeper if the illusion was complete; I had expected that the children would be able to dissociate this from their belief quite simply, but whenever the tape recorder was obvious the children were puzzled and occasionally distracted. This may have been because they were in a half-world where they had not been told whether it was real or drama, but on the other hand they seemed to be able to accept this quite easily. The least satisfactory performances were with two of the control classes, when the actor/teacher introduced himself first—to dissociate the actor from the character was more than some of them could manage.

There were some unsatisfactory details—such as the clue cards, which were too small to be a satisfactory pay-off for the children when they had put them together, and the spaceship, which once or twice became too interesting as a toy in itself, where there was a lot of apparatus, to play with. Overall, the programme seemed to work quite well, though perhaps it was not really stretching enough for the older children; seven years old seemed to be exactly the right age. For most of the children The Pest was the highlight, especially after the emphasis changed from his badness to his mischievousness; he became a potent symbol, often taking on a life of his own in the fantasies of the children after the performance. Some of the plans they suggested and put into operation for dealing with him were:

(a) catching him under the hat by the lure of a sweet;
(b) singing a song for and about him—this proved the most-suggested ending;
(c) singing a scary song to frighten him away;
(d) pretending to be monsters to frighten him away;
(e) making The Pest a guitar of his own so that he would not be jealous of Fred's;
(f) borrowing some pepper from the dinner ladies to make him sneeze and go away;
(g) asking the Head to put the television on for him to watch during the singing;
(h) getting out some books from the book corner for The Pest to read;
(i) luring him outside by telling him jokes, then losing him in the school grounds;
(j) making another journey to The Hall of Pretend to sing the songs there. (When this happened, the Songman went off after the song, saying, 'I'm staying here, where The Pest won't bother me.' Significantly, the children, alone and on their own initiative, all climbed back into the space machine to go back to their own hall, to finish off properly. The teacher, with magnificent aplomb, managed to find the right sound effect, and then give them a touch of The Pest's laughter when they arrived, as a gratuitous thrill—these children were very confident and could cope with it!)

It is quite possible that these results are untrustworthy, unreliable and wrong. If they have any validity, they appear greatly to supplement, almost contradict, the findings of the experiment mentioned at the beginning of this appendix, which may be found in *Outlook* (Annual Journal of the British Children's Theatre Association), Volume 4 (1972), 'Children as Audience', by John Coultas and John Pick.

This apparent contradiction would certainly seem to lend weight to the supposition, which I now offer as a theory, that total integral participation, where the children operate throughout as a group, actually enhances their comprehension of the story; programmes which give the opportunity for a more individualistic contribution, with children involved alone or in small groups, may well create a deeper personal experience, but leave them with a less clear and balanced over-all view. The resulting difference in response, at least as far as it has now been measured, is a factor that perhaps needs bearing strongly in mind in the preparation of programmes, according to the programme's intention. Both methods of involvement seem to me to offer a more profound experience than a purely visual or auditory storytelling, but then I have already set my foot behind the flag of integral participation, as practised by those who know what they are doing, and why they are doing it.

References

* This programme was conceived as 'children's theatre', or 'young people's theatre', not specifically as theatre in education.

† It would not be fair to name this programme because I may well have misunderstood or misrepresented its intention, and I am merely using it as an example of a weakness applicable to many programmes.

1 *The Happy Land* (Durham TIE, 1970).

2 *Ghost in the Village* (Durham TIE, 1974).

3 *The Ballad of Billy Martin* (Durham TIE, 1973).

4 *The Belgrade's Bones* (1970) and *New Directions* (1972) Annual reports of Coventry Belgrade TIE.

5 *The Fire of London* (Flintshire TIE, 1972).

6 *The Day of Fire* (Durham TIE, 1972).

7 *The Butterfly Ball* (Berkshire College of Education, 1972).

8 Tyler, G. (1969) 'Open Letter to the Arts Council of Great Britain', in *Outlook* (Annual Journal of the British Children's Theatre Association), Vol. 1.

9 *The Eagle, the Snake and the Cactus* (Billingham Forum YPT, 1974).

10 Dodd, N. and Hickson, W. (eds.) (1971) *Drama and Theatre in Education*. London: Heinemann Educational.

11 Illich, I. (1971) *Deschooling Society*. London: Calder and Boyars.
Reimer, E. (1971) *School is Dead*. Harmondsworth: Penguin Books.

12 Freire, P. (1972) *The Pedagogy of the Oppressed*. London: Sheed and Ward.

13 Walford, R. (1970) *Games in Geography*. Harlow: Longman.

14 Chorley, R. J. and Huggett, P. (1967) *Models in Geography*. London: Methuen.

15 *Out of the Casebook* (Durham TIE (the author), 1974).

16 *The Belgrade's Bones* (see 4, above).

17 *The Songman and The Pest* (Durham TIE (the author), 1974).

18 Untitled programme for ten- and eleven-year-olds, prepared by Sixth Form College students (1973).

19 Dilworth, M. (1973) *Imagination and Drama*. Unpublished dissertation, University of Durham.

20 *The Story of Jonathan Strong* (Newcastle Stagecoach, 1973).

21 *Snap out of It* (Leeds Playhouse TIE, 1972).
22 *You can't do That* (Newcastle Stagecoach, 1973).
23 Bruner, J. S., *et al.* (1966) *Learning about Learning: A conference report*. Washington, D.C.: US Department of Education.
24 *Beowulf* (Newcastle Stagecoach, 1973).
25 Programme designed by Alsager College of Education students (1972).
26 *A Hook, a Bob and a Four-letter Name* (Greenwich Bowsprit TIE, 1974).
27 *The Cullen Family* (Live Theatre, 1974).
28 *Elaine* (Durham University AD students, 1971).
29 *The Broken Doll* (Newcastle University PGCE students, 1974).
30 The other was by Stockton Dovecot Arts Centre TIE (1972).
31 Key Perspectives TIE, Peterborough and Durham TIE (1973).
32 *What shall we do with Mary?* (Durham TIE (unfinished), 1972).
33 *Simple Simon* (Flintshire TIE, 1973).
34 *The Princess, the Sweep and the Pedlar* (Greenwich Bowsprit TIE, 1973).
35 *Frogs begin at Calais* (Oxford Playhouse Team TIE, 1973).
36 *Syrca Sulwen* (Flintshire TIE, 1972).
37 *New Pence for Old* (Bolton Octagon TIE, 1971).
38 *Are you There* (etc.) (Curved Space Theatre, 1973).
39 *The Bolton Massacre* (Bolton Octagon TIE, 1969).
40 Programme prepared by the Abbey Theatre, Dublin, TIE (1971).
41 *There was an Old Fellow called Bede* (Newcastle Stagecoach, 1973).
42 Two programmes: *The Carmakers* and *Made in Coventry* (Coventry Belgrade TIE, 1971).
43 *Play with Fire* (Newcastle Stagecoach, 1970).
44 Back-up programme by Leeds Playhouse TIE (1972).
45 Programme prepared by Alsager College of Education students (1972).
46 *I Say* (Leeds Playhouse TIE, 1973).
47 *The Global Village Daily News* (Coventry Belgrade TIE, 1971).
48 *The Inventors* (Coventry Belgrade TIE, 1971).
49 Untitled programme by Durham University AD students (1973).
50 Untitled programme by Durham University AD students (1969).
51 *The King's Picture* (Durham University AD students, 1973).
52 Chapman, R. (1972) Speech to Conference of the Council of Repertory Theatres.
53 Dudley, J. (1973) Unpublished dissertation, University of Keele.
54 *The Oddballs* (Coventry Belgrade TIE, 1971).
55 *New Directions* (1972) Coventry Belgrade TIE annual report.

56 *Hare from SCARE* (Greenwich Bowsprit TIE, 1973).

57 *The Lambton Worm* (Stockton Dovecot Arts Centre TIE, 1973).

58 *Who's all right, Jack?* (Cockpit TIE, London, 1974).

59 *Ice Station Zero One* (Coventry Belgrade TIE, 1974).

60 Taylor, J. and Walford, R. (1972) *Simulation in the Classroom*. Harmondsworth: Penguin Books.

61 *What do you do when the Docks ain't Docks?* (Greenwich Bowsprit TIE, 1974).

62 Bruner, J. S. (1966) *Towards a Theory of Instruction*. Cambridge, Mass.: Harvard University Press.

63 Bolton, G. (1973) 'Moral Responsibility in Children's Theatre', in *Outlook* (Annual Journal of the British Children's Theatre Association), Vol. 5.

64 *The Net* (Coventry Belgrade TIE, 1971).

65 Bentley, E. (1965) *The Life of the Drama*. London: Methuen.

66 Davidson, A. and Fay, J. (1972) *Fantasy in Childhood*. Westport, Conn.: Greenwood Press.

67 *How do you swim on Concrete?* (South Tyneside TIE, 1974).

68 *Gremlin* (Bolton Octagon TIE, 1972).

69 Slade, P. (1969) *Experience of Spontaneity*. Harlow: Longman.

70 *Sweetie Pie* (Bolton Octagon TIE, 1972).

71 *This Rare Earth* (Coventry Belgrade TIE, 1973–4).

72 Tyler, G. (1970) Letter to the Editor, in *Outlook* (Annual Journal of the British Children's Theatre Association), Vol. 2.

73 ATO/DES course, Durham University Institute of Education (1973).

74 Tansey, P. J. and Unwin, D. (1969) *Simulation and Gaming in Education*. London: Methuen.

75 (*a*) Priority Everyman Community Theatre, Liverpool (Gulbenkian Foundation);
(*b*) Sunderland Community Theatre (Department of the Environment Quality of Life Experiment).

76 *Holland New Town* (Bolton Octagon TIE, 1974).

77 Prospectus, Octagon Theatre in Education, Bolton, 1973.

78 *Tom Tiddler's Ground* (Flintshire TIE, 1972).

79 Coultas, J. and Pick, J. (1972) 'Children as Audience', in *Outlook* (Annual Journal of the British Children's Theatre Association), Vol. 4.

Further reading

Allen, J. (1968) *Drama in Education* (Department of Education and Science Report No. 50). London: Her Majesty's Stationery Office.

Argyle, M. (1970) *The Psychology of Interpersonal Behaviour*. Harmondsworth: Penguin Books.

B.B.C. (1972) *Games and Simulations*. London: B.B.C. Publications.

Burns, E. (1972) *Theatricality*. Harlow: Longman.

Cass, J. (1971) *The Significance of Children's Play*. London: Batsford.

Courtney, R. (1968) *Play, Drama and Thought*. London: Cassell.

Davidson, A. and Fay, J. (1972) *Fantasy in Childhood*. Westport, Conn.: Greenwood Press.

Davis, J. H. and Watkins, M. J. (1960) *Children's Theatre*. New York: Harper and Row.

English in Education (1967) Vol. 1, No. 3. National Association for the Teaching of English.

Fines, J. and Verrier, R. (1975) *The Drama of History*. London: Clive Bingley.

Goffman, E. (1971) *The Presentation of Self in Everyday Life*. Harmondsworth: Penguin Books.

Hartley, R. E., *et al.* (1952) *Understanding Children's Play*. New York: Columbia University Press.

Hodgson, J. and Banham, M. (1974) *Drama in Education, Volume 3*. London: Pitman.

Holbrook, D. (1957) *Children's Games*. London: Gordon Fraser.

Jennings, S. (1973) *Remedial Drama*. London: Pitman.

Jones, A. and Buttrey, J. (1971) *Children and Stories*. Oxford: Blackwell.

Male, D. (1973) *Approaches to Drama*. London: Allen and Unwin.

Masefield, P. (1975) *Theatre Provision for Young People on Merseyside*. Merseyside Arts Association.

Millar, S. (1971) *The Psychology of Play*. Harmondsworth: Penguin Books.

Opie, I. and P. (1959) *The Lore and Language of Schoolchildren*. Oxford: Clarendon Press.

Opie, I. and P. (1969) *Children's Games in Street and Playground*. Oxford: Clarendon Press.

Postman, N. and Weingartner, C. (1971) *Teaching as a Subversive Activity*. Harmondsworth: Penguin Books.

Slade, P. (1954) *Child Drama*. London: Hodder and Stoughton.

Way, B. (1967) *Development through Drama*. London: Longmans.

Index